The Voice of Reason

The Voice of Reason offers a refreshing and practical take on the craft of judgment writing. Reflective yet firmly grounded in experience, it draws on the author's dual vantage point as a sitting judge and seasoned judicial educator, shaped by more than a decade of developing judgment writing programmes and tools.

The book explains why, for whom, and how judges ought to write and distils the qualities of effective judicial prose – robustness, tightness, precision, and concision, and a tone marked by respect and humility. It provides practical judgment writing tips, while also confronting the emerging challenges of digital readership and the responsible use of artificial intelligence in judgment writing.

Designed for all who craft judicial reasons – judges, judicial officers, tribunal members, and arbitrators – the book speaks to both new and experienced writers. Drawing on international jurisprudence and offering the first sustained treatment of judgment writing enriched by examples from Singapore case law, it adopts a global orientation that invites readers to refine their craft in service of what every judgment must ultimately embody: the voice of reason.

Justin Yeo is the Executive Director of the Singapore Judicial College and a District Judge in Singapore.

JUSTIN YEO

The Voice of Reason

On the Craft of Judgment Writing

Routledge
Taylor & Francis Group
LONDON AND NEW YORK

Designed cover image: cover concept by Justin Yeo and Leong Shenqyu; photograph by Colin Seow; digital compositing by Jolene Yeo.

First published 2027
by Routledge
4 Park Square, Milton Park, Abingdon, Oxon OX14 4RN

and by Routledge
605 Third Avenue, New York, NY 10158

Routledge is an imprint of the Taylor & Francis Group, an informa business

British Library Cataloguing-in-Publication Data
A catalogue record for this book is available from the British Library

Library of Congress Cataloging-in-Publication Data
Names: Yeo, Justin author
Title: The voice of reason : on the craft of judgment writing / Justin Yeo.
Description: New York : Routledge, 2026. | Includes bibliographical references and index. | Summary: — Provided by publisher.
Identifiers: LCCN 2026030085 (print) | LCCN 2026030086 (ebook) | ISBN 9781041392392 hardback | ISBN 9781041392378 paperback | ISBN 9781042017027 ebook
Subjects: LCSH: Judgments—Authorship | Legal composition
Classification: LCC K487.L36 Y46 2026 (print) | LCC K487.L36 (ebook)
LC record available at https://lccn.loc.gov/2026030085
LC ebook record available at https://lccn.loc.gov/2026030086

ISBN: 978-1-041-39239-2 (hbk)
ISBN: 978-1-041-39237-8 (pbk)
ISBN: 978-1-042-01702-7 (ebk)

DOI: 10.4324/9781042017027

Typeset in Joanna
by Apex CoVantage, LLC

To those who serve justice with a reasoned voice,
and to my family – Shengyu and Royce.

Contents

Foreword

Judges are entrusted with the weighty task of sitting in judgment over the affairs of others. This duty calls for not only legal acumen but also a matrix of qualities that are easier to name than to cultivate: among them, the courage to choose principle over power, the compassion to recognise the people behind the parties, and the humility to be persuaded against one's initial point of view.

The written judgment is the principal artefact through which all of this becomes visible. It is how a court accounts for its decision to the parties and submits its reasoning to scrutiny. It is how the enterprise of adjudication is made intelligible to the wider community, whose acceptance of judicial decisions ultimately sustains the legitimacy of the courts. A judgment does not merely memorialise an outcome; it encapsulates the very process by which that outcome was reached. As the author pithily puts it, a judgment should be transformed 'from a record of thought into a demonstration of thought'.

This emphasis on process matters for at least three reasons. First, a judgment is the best evidence that a judge has discharged his foremost duty of judicious consideration – that the decision reached was founded on reason, following a fair, diligent and careful consideration of all the material before the court. It is by engaging thoughtfully with the arguments of the parties, including those that failed to gain purchase, that the judge provides the surest assurance that all parties have received a fair hearing. Second, the process of writing tends to improve the decision itself. The discipline of putting pen to paper forces the writer to confront gaps and assumptions that might otherwise have been smoothed over in the writer's mind. In this sense, judgment writing is as much an act of authorship as it is a continuing exercise of judgment. Third, to write a judgment is to do more than to dispose of the immediate dispute; it is also to participate in the wider project of developing the law. Reasoned judgments provide markers that chart the path along which the common law travels. In many cases, the precedents they set and the principles they articulate serve as beacons that illuminate the way forward and guide those who follow.

All of this is to say that judgment writing is no small undertaking. To ensure that it is done well, it ought to be approached as a craft. It must be honed with intentionality, through serious practice, sustained reflection, and a sincere desire to perfect one's technique.

The Voice of Reason takes up this craft. It is a book that marries the 'why' and the 'how' of judgment writing – a practical guide anchored in a principled account of why judgment writing matters. And, as its title suggests, it returns on several occasions to the deeper question of the *judicial voice*. Three threads of that discussion are worth distilling, as a preview of the far richer treatment to be found in the book itself.

The first is the aphorism that words carry weight. The words that judges choose shape how justice is seen to be done and how it is felt by those subject to it. The author shows, for instance, how rhetorical flourish can distract from the reasoning it is meant to ornament; how 'judicial ventriloquism' (or parroting a party's submissions) can erode the perception of judicial impartiality and faith in the judicial process; but also how well-chosen words of disapproval can register the gravity of misconduct with fitting force. To compose a judgment is to make dozens of such decisions on form, construction, and register, and it is their cumulative effect that gives the judgment its authority and its character.

The second thread is the reminder that judgments should be written with the reader in mind. The reader, the author observes, is rarely a single audience but several at once: the parties, the public, the press, the profession, and posterity. Each reads through a different prism, and an effective judgment should hold all of them in view. Judges should use their voice not to impress but to express; not merely to sound intelligent but to be intelligible. The author unpacks a suite of techniques in service of this reader-centric discipline, such as pruning linguistic clutter, setting up structural scaffolds, responding to modern reading habits, and writing simply without being simplistic.

The third thread is the call to preserve the *human* voice in judgment writing. The book confronts a number of contemporary challenges to the established traditions of judgment writing, the most profound of which is perhaps the rise of generative artificial intelligence ('AI') and its remarkable capacity to simulate legal writing and analysis. The author offers perspectives on this topic that are both principled and practical. He weighs candidly the opportunities and risks that AI brings to the work of judgment writing, and lands on a position of measured caution – a set of six best practices that, in his vivid framing, will help judges remain 'Centaurs' rather than 'Cyborgs' in a world of AI.

Written with eloquence, rigour, and a welcome dose of levity, this book is more than a manual on judgment writing. It is a meditation on judging as a craft, by an author who has plainly thought long and hard about that craft and who has spent many years refining his own, both as a judge and as a judicial educator. The book demystifies many of the finer aspects of judgecraft, drawing its insights from a wide range of international jurisprudence and, distinctively, from a substantial body of Singapore decisions. It will serve as an accessible introduction for those new to the discipline and as a precious repository of techniques and reflections that will resonate with more seasoned hands. I congratulate the author on this excellent publication, and warmly commend it to fellow judges, judicial officers, arbitrators, educators, and indeed to all who share in the responsibility of administering justice and in the privilege of giving reasons in its pursuit.

Sundaresh Menon
Chief Justice
Supreme Court of Singapore

Acknowledgements

Writing about judgment writing requires a similar discipline to the craft itself: deciding what to emphasise, what to omit, and how best to serve the reader's needs. This book has been shaped by the guidance and generosity of those who have helped me navigate those choices.

I owe a particular debt to Chief Justice Sundaresh Menon, whose encouragement and support set me on the path of exploring and teaching the craft of judgment writing more than a decade ago. His leadership has profoundly shaped my thinking, and I am deeply honoured that he has written the Foreword to this book.

I am grateful to Justice Rosalie Abella, Justice Andrew Phang, Justice Kwek Mean Luck, Professor Natalie Skead, and two anonymous reviewers for reading the manuscript and offering invaluable comments that have strengthened this book in many important ways. I also thank Mr Yeong Zee Kin for sharing his expertise and perspectives on the technology-related chapters (i.e., Chapters 7 and 8). My thanks go as well to District Judge Reuben Ong and Ms Andrea Ong for their suggestions, their contributions to research and ideas, and their meticulous work in ensuring the accuracy and coherence of the manuscript. They offered their time and diligence with a commitment that far exceeded anything I could have asked.

I have learned much from the many batches of participants at the Singapore Judicial College's Judgment Writing 101 programme. Their questions, challenges, and reflections have sharpened my thinking and pushed me not just to refine the substantive content but also to deliver it in engaging ways. Interacting with them has helped me better understand how judges find, develop, and strengthen their own judicial voices.

I express my gratitude to the team at Routledge for their professionalism and dedication in bringing this book to fruition; to Mr Colin Seow for capturing the photograph that realises the cover concept; and to Ms Jolene Yeo for her artful digital compositing of that photograph.

Finally, I thank my family – Shengyu and Royce – for their love, patience, and understanding throughout the writing of this book. Shengyu contributed creatively to the book cover and also provided the quiet support and encouragement that made the book possible. Royce, who is far from quiet, contributed much joy – and the spark behind the scene that introduces Chapter 3.

This book is offered in my personal capacity and is not intended to convey the views of any institution I have served or am serving. Any errors in these pages are mine alone – they evidently survived my best efforts in applying the revision and review principles advocated in this book.

About the Author

Justin Yeo is the Executive Director of the Singapore Judicial College and a District Judge in Singapore. He graduated as valedictorian from the National University of Singapore (Bachelor of Laws, First Class Honours) and holds a Master of Laws from Harvard Law School. He has served as justices' law clerk and Assistant Registrar at the Singapore Supreme Court, Deputy Divisional Registrar of Singapore's two highest appellate courts, and Counsel for Parliamentary Affairs at Singapore's Ministry of Law. Recognised as the 'Most Outstanding Adjunct' faculty member at Singapore Management University's Yong Pung How School of Law, he brings a longstanding passion for teaching to the judicial education space. He has taught judgment writing internationally to judges and adjudicators from both common law and civil law traditions – a breadth that enriches *The Voice of Reason*.

by Colin Seow.

Table of Cases

Australia

Beale v Government Insurance Office of NSW (1997) 48 NSWLR 430 (NSWCA)
Green v Green (1989) 17 NSWLR 343 (NSWCA)
Pettitt v Dunkley [1971] 1 NSWLR 376 (NSWCA)
Sun Alliance Insurance Ltd v Massoud [1989] VR 8 (Supreme Court of Victoria)

England and Wales

Capital and Suburban Properties Ltd v Swycher [1976] Ch 319 (CA)
Coleman v Dunlop Ltd (CA, 26 November 1997)
Dallah Real Estate and Tourism Holding Co v Ministry of Religious Affairs of the Government of Pakistan [2010] UKSC 46, [2011] 1 AC 763
Donoghue v Stevenson [1932] AC 562 (HL)
Eagil Trust Co Ltd v Pigott-Brown [1985] 3 All ER 119 (CA)
Edgington v Fitzmaurice (1885) 29 Ch D 459 (CA)
Gollins v Gollins [1963] UKHL 5, [1964] AC 644
Healthcare at Home Ltd v Common Services Agency [2014] UKSC 49
Knight v Clifton [1971] Ch 700 (CA)
Miller v Jackson [1977] QB 966 (CA)

New Zealand

Connell v Auckland City Council [1977] 1 NZLR 630 (NZHC)

Singapore

Aljunied-Hougang Town Council v Lim Swee Lian Sylvia [2019] SGHC 241
Ayaz Ahmad v Mustaq Ahmad @ Mushtaq Ahmad s/o Mustafa [2022] SGHC 241
DNZ v DOA [2026] SGHC(I) 1

Eugene Phoa (personal representative of the estate of Evelyn Phoa @ Lauw, Evelyn Siew Chiang, deceased, and personal representative of the estate of William Phoa, deceased) v Oey Liang Ho @ Henry Kasenda (sole executor of the estate of Wirio Kasenda @ Oey Giok Tjeng, deceased) [2024] SGHC 22
Foo Jee Seng v Foo Jhee Tuang [2012] SGCA 41, [2012] 4 SLR 339
Gillingham James Ian v Fearless Legends Pte Ltd [2023] SGHCR 13
Goh Guan Sin (by her litigation representative Chiam Yu Zhu) v Yeo Tseng Tsai [2019] SGHC 274, [2021] 3 SLR 364
How Weng Fan v Sengkang Town Council [2022] SGCA 72, [2023] 1 SLR 707
Hyatt Terminal and Industrial Corp v Filipinas Third Millenium Realty Corp [2026] SGHC(I) 3
IIa Technologies Pte Ltd v Element Six Technologies Ltd [2023] SGCA 5, [2023] 1 SLR 987
Imran bin Mohd Arip v Public Prosecutor [2021] SGCA 91, [2021] 2 SLR 1198
L Capital Jones Ltd v Maniach Pte Ltd
Ler Chun Poh v Public Prosecutor [2024] SGHC 307, [2024] 6 SLR 410
Lim Chee Huat v Public Prosecutor [2019] SGHC 132, [2019] 5 SLR 433
Love & Co Pte Ltd v The Carat Club Pte Ltd [2008] SGHC 158, [2009] 1 SLR(R) 561
Mak-Levrion Kah Kay Natasha (alias Mai Jiaqi Natasha) v R Shiamala [2023] SGHC 335, [2024] 4 SLR 616
Man Financial (S) Pte Ltd v Wong Bark Chuan David [2007] SGCA 53, [2008] 1 SLR(R) 663
Newton David Christopher v Public Prosecutor [2023] SGHC 266, [2024] 3 SLR 1370
Parakou Investment Holdings Pte Ltd v Parakou Shipping Pte Ltd (in liquidation) [2018] SGCA 3, [2018] 1 SLR 271
Public Prosecutor v Gaiyathiri d/o Murugayan [2021] SGHC 187, [2022] 4 SLR 560
Public Prosecutor v GMS Carwerkz [2026] SGMC 15
Public Prosecutor v Henry Koh Yik Wee [2025] SGMC 64
Public Prosecutor v Pang Shuo [2016] SGHC 82, [2016] 3 SLR 903
Public Prosecutor v Ridhaudin Ridhwan bin Bakri [2019] SGHC 105
Public Prosecutor v Soh Chee Wen [2023] SGHC 299
Public Prosecutor v Takaaki Masui [2021] SGCA 119, [2022] 1 SLR 1033

Public Prosecutor v Thong Ah Fat [2010] SGHC 227
Quoine Pte Ltd v B2C2 Ltd [2020] SGCA(I) 2, [2020] 2 SLR 20
RDC Concrete Pte Ltd v Sato Kogyo (S) Pte Ltd [2007] SGCA 39, [2007] 4 SLR(R) 413
Ripon v Public Prosecutor [2022] SGHC 255, [2023] 3 SLR 896
See Fong Mun v Chan Yuen Lan [2013] SGHC 99, [2013] 3 SLR 685
Syed Fathuddin Putra bin Syed A Rahman v Public Prosecutor [2023] SGHC 338, [2024] 3 SLR 1672
Tajudin bin Gulam Rasul v Suriaya bte Haja Mohideen [2025] SGHCR 33
Takaaki Masui v Public Prosecutor [2020] SGHC 265, [2021] 4 SLR 160
Tan Cheng Bock v Attorney-General [2017] SGCA 50, [2017] 2 SLR 850
Tan Hai Peng Micheal and another v Tan Cheong Joo and another [2026] SGHC 49
Thong Ah Fat v Public Prosecutor [2011] SGCA 65, [2012] 1 SLR 676
Vasentha d/o Joseph v Public Prosecutor [2015] SGHC 197, [2015] 5 SLR 122
Yap Ah Lai v Public Prosecutor [2014] SGHC 70, [2014] 3 SLR 180

United States

Berkey v Third Avenue Railway Co 244 NY 84, 155 NE 58 (NY 1926)
Fisher v Lowe 122 Mich App 418, 333 NW2d 67 (Mich Ct App 1983)
Gonzalez-Servin v Ford Motor Co 662 F3d 931 (7th Cir 2011)
Mata v Avianca, Inc 678 F Supp 3d 443 (SDNY 2023)
Productos Carnic SA v Central American Beef and Seafood Trading Co 621 F2d 683 (5th Cir 1980)
Ross v United States (District of Columbia Court of Appeals, 20 February 2025)
Russell v State 372 SE2d 445 (Ga Ct App 1988)
Snell v United Specialty Insurance Company 102 F4th 1208 (11th Cir 2024)
Stock v Commissioner 551 F 2d 614, 615 (5th Cir 1977).
Wheat v Fraker 107 Ga App 318 (1963)

Preface

The Voice of Reason

Early in my legal career, I served as a justices' law clerk at the Supreme Court of Singapore. One of my key responsibilities was to assist the Supreme Court judges with drafting judgments. In a particularly complex and controversial case before the Court of Appeal – Singapore's apex court – I experienced first-hand how demanding the writing process could be, especially when clarity and structure (and repeated refinements) were most needed. The case would later become a *locus classicus* in its field, but what struck me at the time was something less legally intellectual: the tools available for structuring and drafting judgments, though serviceable, had much room for improvement. That observation prompted a personal experiment – to develop a structured, technology-enabled word-processing template designed to make the judgment writing process more fluid, more coherent, less prone to error, and capable of producing results that are not only professional but also elegant in form. The resulting template remains in use across all levels of court in Singapore today, periodically refined to meet evolving needs.

That experience sparked a lasting interest in the craft of judgment writing. As I assumed judicial office, where writing judgments became a regular part of my work, I continued to explore how to write judgments better, and how to write better judgments.

A major step in this journey came in 2015 when, on the request of the Chief Justice of the Dubai International Financial Centre ('DIFC') Courts Michael Hwang, Chief Justice of Singapore Sundaresh Menon entrusted me with developing a two-day crash course on common law judgment writing for the DIFC Courts' judicial officers who came from the civil law tradition. I leapt at the opportunity. By then, I had already accumulated formal teaching experience as an adjunct lecturer at a university, and I assumed – perhaps too readily – that my personal interest and experience in judgment writing would make the task straightforward.

How wrong I was. Developing this judgment writing programme forced me to confront questions I had never consciously examined – not

DOI: 10.4324/9781042017027-1

just *how* we write judgments in the common law, but *why* we write them the way we do. I considered various texts, one of the most influential being an earlier edition of Professor Edward Berry's *Writing Reasons: A Handbook for Judges*. The multitude of books, articles, and speeches I had read while preparing to teach offered a wealth of perspectives and practical guidance. But I also came to see that there was no formulaic way to write a judgment. I therefore began to develop my own thinking and perspectives on judgment writing.

Since then, I have had the privilege of further exploring the craft of judgment writing, especially through my work with the Singapore Judicial College. Through the College, I have taught judgment writing to a large range of judges, judicial officers, and justices' law clerks, quasi-judicial officers or tribunal members, as well as foreign judges. I have also had the opportunity to learn from and teach alongside judgment writing experts from Canada's National Judicial Institute and the Commonwealth Judicial Education Institute. Each of these experiences has deepened my appreciation for the craft and complexity of writing judgments.

As a sitting judge who continues to preside over cases at the time of this writing, I have written many a judgment under time pressure. I have wrestled with structure and tone, written across mealtimes and late into the night, and wondered whether I had done justice and properly conveyed so in writing. This has helped me appreciate better the rigour of analysis, the weight of words, and the quiet discipline required to hone what I have come to think of as the voice of reason.

This book builds upon my experience in judgment writing, and in teaching it. It is a series of reflections drawn from experience, shaped by teaching, and grounded in the belief that judgment writing is not just a skill, but a responsibility. While it is not a textbook, handbook, workbook, or manual (for there are already publications available that cover the technical details), judgment writing cannot be meaningfully discussed without touching on certain practical elements that are integral to the craft. For this reason, I have included a small number of carefully curated practical suggestions and writing 'hacks' – not a comprehensive catalogue of writing techniques, but foundational methods that can serve as springboards for further exploration as each judge develops a personal approach to the craft. My hope is that this book helps those who write judgments – whether new to the task or seasoned in it – to pause, reflect, and refine their craft.

Judgment writing is the most visible form of judicial reasoning. It is how judges explain, persuade, and account for the power we exercise. It must reflect deliberation, restraint, and care. It must be principled, measured, and authentic. It must speak not only to the parties but also to the public; not only to the present but also to posterity. It must be more than a record of decision. It must stand, above all, as the voice of reason.

The Written Judgment – Why, Who, How

One

On 12 June 2025, Air India Flight AI171 – a London-bound Boeing 787 Dreamliner – crashed into a residential complex in Ahmedabad just moments after take-off. The tragedy claimed at least 270 lives.[1] In the days that followed, investigators combed through the wreckage, hoping to recover two small devices: the Enhanced Airborne Flight Recorders, commonly known as 'black boxes'.[2]

Despite their name, black boxes are not black (although they were when introduced during World War II). They are painted bright orange to be more visible in the aftermath of the accident.[3] One black box records cockpit voices; the other, flight data. Together, they capture the final moments of the flight – altitude, speed, alarms, pilot conversations, and control inputs. They do not prevent the incident, but they help explain it. They tell the story of *what* happened and *how* it happened. They are thus not just records of action, but instruments of accountability. They exist not only for the investigators but also for the families, the regulators, and the public.

A properly reasoned written judgment is the 'black box' of judicial decision-making. It captures not just the outcome of the judicial decision but also *what* happened and *how* it happened: the facts considered, the law applied, and the reasoning that led to the conclusion.

A poorly written (or poorly reasoned) judgment, or the absence of reasons altogether, brings to mind a different type of 'black box' – the version as understood in the fields of science and computing, that is, 'a system that produces results without the user being able to see or understand how it works'.[4] Such a judgment is sealed and opaque. The parties may know the result, but not the rationale. The public may see the outcome, but not the process.

This book is an attempt to explore how our written judgments can serve as a 'black box' in the aviation sense. It begins by asking three questions in this opening chapter: *why* do we write judgments, for *whom* do we write, and *how* should we write them? These are not abstract inquiries. They shape what we prioritise and how we understand the

DOI: 10.4324/9781042017027-2

responsibilities of authorship. Writing is, after all, the most visible and enduring expression of the voice of reason.

WHY DO WE WRITE?

The idea that judges should explain their decisions is not as self-evident as it may seem. There was a time when courts routinely withheld their reasoning.

In pre-modern continental Europe, Roman, ecclesiastical, and aristocratic courts often functioned without giving reasons. Their task was to decide cases, not to explain them. The College of Pontiffs in Ancient Rome issued legal pronouncements without offering explanations.[5] Indeed, the term 'pontificate', initially a neutral expression derived from the Medieval Latin *pontifex* (meaning 'to officiate as a pontiff'), subsequently acquired derisive connotations such as an air of 'spurious superiority' or unwarranted authority.[6] In the 12th and 13th centuries, explaining decisions was thought to jeopardise the power and legitimacy of the courts.[7] Reason-giving could create the appearance of uncertainty and invite criticism – not only by litigants but also by other powerful institutions, including royal power.[8] By refraining from giving reasons, the courts preserved their discretion and insulated their decisions from review, in a manner somewhat akin to modern practices in the context of jury deliberations, political voting, clemency decisions, and matters relating to national security.[9]

During the French Revolution in the late 18th century, revolutionary reforms required courts to provide reasons for their decisions. This was not so much to promote transparency as it was to constrain judicial power of the courts of the day, which were generally seen as corrupt and an enemy of reform.[10] With these reforms, judges were no longer to participate in lawmaking; instead, legislation would be the primary source of law. The requirement to give reasons was intended to ensure that decisions could be traced to legislative authority (think: legislative supremacy) and that the judges could be monitored.[11] Ironically, this gave rise to a 'cryptic style of opinion writing', so much so that these judges were arguably less constrained than their common law counterparts.[12] Indeed, the French judicial opinion of this era has been described as 'an uninformative syllogism of a few hundred words that purports to deduce the holding from a code or statutory provision'[13] – a piece of writing that '[lacks] any developed findings of fact, almost never [refers] to past judicial decisions, and [contains] little that could be considered as serious interpretive or policy analysis'.[14] In other words, the reason-giving requirement was hardly an effective check on judicial decision-making.[15]

Even in the common law tradition, where judge-made law has long been central, the value of reason-giving was not always embraced in certain contexts. Lord Mansfield, often regarded as one of the greatest British jurists of the 18th century and the founder of English commercial law,[16] reportedly advised: 'never give your reasons; for your judgment will probably be right, but your reasons will certainly be wrong'.[17] For context, this piece of advice was given to an army officer appointed as governor of an island in the West Indies (who had no legal training and had never appeared in a court of justice in his life).[18] It was, perhaps, a pragmatic concession to the risks of overreaching in unfamiliar terrain. In any event, as the Singapore Court of Appeal observed in the decision of *Thong Ah Fat v Public Prosecutor* (the first Singapore case exploring, in detail, the judicial duty to give reasons[19]), Lord Mansfield's advice would today be 'regarded as judicial heresy and inimical to sound judicial practice'.[20] Put another way, the age of judicial pontification (if there was one) has well and truly passed. Indeed, at least since the 20th century, common law courts all around the world have emphasised the importance – and even expectation – of common law judges providing reasons for their decisions.[21] It is now 'settled law that a judge must ordinarily give adequate reasons for any decision made',[22] although there are exceptions such as where the factual or legal issues are so straightforward that the reasons for the decision may be easily inferred,[23] where the matters in question do not bear directly on substantive matters (such as interlocutory applications with a procedural focus,[24] or where a judge exercises discretion in awarding a usual award of costs[25]).

It is important to highlight, at this juncture, the distinction between what has been called the 'duty to give reasons' and the duty to issue *written* judgments. The former does not necessitate the latter. In this regard, it is well recognised that 'reasons can be provided orally where appropriate',[26] such as where the volume or nature of cases renders written judgments impractical (e.g., where sentencing courts are making sentencing decisions based on established sentencing benchmarks[27]).

In the remainder of this section, I explore four fundamental reasons for giving judicial reasons in general, and *written* reasons in particular: strengthening the rule of law, promoting transparency and accountability, encouraging accuracy, and affirming participation and respect.

Strengthening the Rule of Law

Giving (written) reasons plays a critical role in strengthening the rule of law. A written judgment allows the parties to understand why they have won or lost.[28] This assures them that the decision was made by a neutral judicial mind engaged in reasoned deliberation and in accordance with the law rather than arbitrary assertion. It facilitates any available right of appeal, ensuring that judicial reasoning can be scrutinised by a higher tribunal, and that errors (if any) can be corrected.[29] It also reinforces the principle that the law is applied equally to all.

Written reasons also systemically strengthen the rule of law beyond the individual case. They contribute to the clarity, consistency, and accessibility of the law not just to the parties but to all stakeholders within a justice system.[30] Professor Lon Fuller, in his classic *The Morality of Law*, identified eight principles that form the 'inner morality' of a legal system: that laws must be general, public, prospective, clear, consistent, practicable, stable, and congruent.[31] Written judgments are important contributions towards realising these ideals because they guide subjects of the law (i.e., the people) on the legal process and the range of legally permissible (or impermissible) actions.[32] They demonstrate how legal rules are interpreted and applied, so that the people know what behaviour is expected of them. They also shape how individuals and institutions conduct themselves in the 'shadow of the law',[33] where contracts are drafted, commercial risks allocated, regulatory strategies designed, divorce settlements negotiated, and even plea bargains negotiated with an eye to the body of judicial reasons that judges produce.[34] Coupled with the doctrine of precedent where applicable, written judgments encourage consistency, uphold the expectations of litigants and the broader community, and thereby serve to reinforce the rule of law.[35]

Promoting Transparency and Accountability

Closely related to strengthening the rule of law is the fact that giving written reasons promotes the transparency and accountability of the judicial system as well as the judge's decision in the specific case.[36]

Judge Learned Hand (one can hardly imagine a better name for a judge;[37] indeed, this is now the name of a generative artificial intelligence platform designed to help judges draft orders[38]) once asked[39]:

> *To whom am I responsible? No one can fire me. No one can dock my pay. Even those nine bozos in Washington, who sometimes reverse me, can't make me decide as they want. Everyone should be responsible to someone. To whom am I responsible?*

He then gestured to a stack of law books:

> *To those books about us! That's to whom I am responsible.*

Referencing the learned judge's (pun intended) comments, a commentator mused: 'how on earth do you address a judicial opinion to "law books"'.[40] My personal reflection on the quote is that despite the judicial independence enjoyed by judges, they must remain and be seen to remain accountable *to the law* – a living body of doctrine, precedent, and principle that transcends individual personalities. After all, judicial independence is not a 'self-serving judicial privilege',[41] but a structural safeguard to ensure that judges can decide cases fairly and free from external pressures (whether political, financial, social, or personal). Its true purpose is to protect the integrity of the judicial process, not the individuals who occupy the bench. Independence without accountability risks arbitrariness, and Judge Learned Hand's gesture to the law books is a vivid metaphor for the need for balance: while judges may not answer to superiors in the conventional sense, they are deeply accountable to the law itself. In this way, accountability is not the antithesis of judicial independence, but its necessary companion.

The written judgment takes on added significance when we recall that judges are generally required to speak only through their judgments and to refrain from publicly commenting on cases once decided.[42] A written judgment is therefore a judge's primary (and often only) opportunity to be transparent about and accountable for the exercise of judicial power.

It is also useful to consider John Rawls' theory of justice and, specifically, his doctrine of public reason. Rawls argued that the giving of reasons for the use of public force is an essential legitimising feature of a liberal democratic state.[43] In this regard, Rawls observed that while legislators and citizens may vote as they wished based on their controversial conceptions of the good:[44]

> *public reason is the sole reason the court exercises. It is the only branch of government that is visibly on its face the creature of that reason and that reason alone.*

How does the giving of reasons help demonstrate the transparency and accountability of the courts?

First, in the context of democratic societies, the giving of reasons ties the exercise of judicial power to prior democratic acts such as legislation and constitutional principles.[45] Judicial reason-giving demonstrates that judges have not departed from the legal framework established by the democratically elected branches of government. It affirms that judicial decisions are not arbitrary or personal, but are grounded in the law as enacted by the legislature and interpreted through constitutional norms. This reinforces the legitimacy of judicial authority by showing that courts are not substituting their own preferences for those of the legislature, but are instead faithfully applying the law within the bounds of their institutional role. Even in non-democratic societies, judicial reason-giving can demonstrate the proper implementation of government and national policies, thus providing a measure of transparency and accountability in the exercise of public power.

Second, the giving of judicial reasons facilitates the judicial and public oversight of judges.[46] They provide a transparent record of how and why decisions are made, enabling scrutiny not only by appellate courts but also by the broader legal community and the public. This transparency takes on an added layer of significance in multi-judge panels, such as appellate and apex courts, where the presence of dissenting or concurring opinions plays a vital role in enriching the judicial discourse. Such dissents or concurrences illuminate the range of legally plausible understandings of the law and highlight the complexity of the issues at hand. In the context of dissents, by articulating alternative reasoning, judges in the minority challenge those in the majority to justify their position more rigorously, thereby strengthening the quality of judicial reasoning. They also enhance internal accountability, as judges must engage with competing views and defend their conclusions in the face of principled disagreement. Dissents have also not infrequently laid the groundwork for future changes to the law.

Third, judicial reasons are the mechanisms through which judges persuade other stakeholders (i.e., litigants, the legal community, and the public) that the court has reached a proper resolution of a dispute. By doing so, the court secures the 'tacit approval and obedience of the governed'.[47]

Fourth, giving judicial reasons ensures that a wide variety of audiences can evaluate, debate, and critique judicial decisions.[48] For instance, it has been observed that written reasons allow an appellate court to have the proper material to understand and to do justice to the first instance decision, rather than having to speculate as to why the judge below decided in a certain way.[49] Written reasons also facilitate and increase public discussions on important points concerning law and governance and societal values. We see this manifesting in the form of discussions in the media, in law schools, around dinner tables, and, in some cases, even sparking 'national debate'.[50]

Encouraging Accuracy

Giving (written) reasons encourages accuracy in decision-making. Writing is not just a means of expression. It is a method of thought, and a safeguard against error.[51] It disciplines the mind, tests assumptions, and reveals gaps in logic. As Justice Anthony Meagher says, '[t]he requirement to provide reasons can operate prophylactically on the judicial mind, guarding against the birth of an unconsidered or impulsive decision'.[52]

Justice Andrew Phang had once shared with me (then, a justices' law clerk who just began clerking for the Singapore Court of Appeal) that if one finds it very difficult to justify a provisional conclusion in writing, one ought to reconsider the correctness of the conclusion. Similarly, Judge Richard Posner has observed that when judges try to systematise a decision in sentences and paragraphs, they may find that what was once a confident conclusion 'will not write'.[53]

Reasoning that seemed sound in the abstract may appear half-baked on the page. This is because writing encourages critical detachment. It forces the judge to pause and ask: 'Does this follow? Is this fair? Have I considered the other side?'

This process enhances accuracy through imposing a form of self-discipline and self-education, thus minimising the risk of misjudgment.[54] Many misconceptions and oversights of fact and law are discovered in the process of writing.[55] Chief Justice of the High Court of Australia Harry Gibbs agreed with Sir Frank Kitto's preference for a judgment to be written rather than given orally, observing:[56]

> *the reasons given for an extemporary judgement have not been tested in the way that the very act of attempting to set out in writing the steps in one's reasoning tests the correctness of one's thinking and reveals any errors that may lurk in it.*

The giving of (written) reasons also helps constrain the space for error by serving as a safeguard against judicial arbitrariness.[57] A judge who must explain a decision, particularly in systematic written form, is less likely to act on impulse or bias. This is because the need to explain the decision limits the range of potential outcomes for a case to those that can be reasonably justified.[58] Requiring decision-makers to explain their reasoning can reduce certain biases – such as confirmation bias (the human tendency to seek information that confirms pre-existing beliefs), anchoring bias (the human tendency to decide based on initial impressions or other arbitrary anchors), and the availability heuristic (the human tendency to rely on 'top of mind' information simply because it is recent, frequent, or memorable).[59] Beyond the immediate case, written decisions also help shape the scope of future exercises of judicial discretion by providing a precedent against which future judges can benchmark their decisions and endeavour to treat like cases alike.[60]

Affirming Participation and Respect

Finally, giving (written) reasons affirms parties' participation in the judicial process and enables the judge to demonstrate respect for the parties whose interests are entrusted to the court.

Professor Lon Fuller defined the essence of adjudication in terms of participation,[61] observing that without reasoned judicial decisions, 'the parties have to take it on faith that their participation in the decision has been real'.[62] To provide a reasoned judgment is to acknowledge that the parties matter, that their arguments were heard, and that their dignity was respected.

Where reasons for the decision are given, a party (usually the losing party) can see that the positions advanced were considered, even if not ultimately accepted by the judge. Where reasons are withheld or insufficiently explained, there may be a lingering suspicion that the judge did not completely understand one's case.[63] There is, after all, a 'world of difference between a disappointed litigant and a disturbed litigant', the latter being one who 'cannot understand why the decision went against him'.[64] Indeed, '[t]o be condemned without being understood is as bad as being condemned unheard'.[65]

Closely related to the participation principle is respect for the parties. This comes to the forefront in certain areas such as family law, where each party may have deep grievances arising from relational difficulties over an extended period, and neither party is completely at 'fault' (so to speak). When the reasons reveal how the judge wrestled with the decision and convey the nuanced balancing that went through the judicial mind, parties are more likely to feel respected and that they have meaningfully participated in the proceedings. Take, for instance, acrimonious divorce proceedings where emotions run deep and where both parties have, in different ways, made meaningful contributions to the family unit. In such cases, a well-reasoned judgment that acknowledges the efforts, sacrifices, and contributions of each parent – in the economic and non-economic (e.g., caregiving) senses – can go a long way in affirming their dignity. When a judge makes the effort to recognise that both parents have sought to provide a loving and stable environment for their children and expresses hope for healing and mutual support moving forward, it signals to the parties that their efforts have been seen and valued. Even if the outcome is not what one party hoped for, the articulation of such reasoning can help that party feel understood and affirmed, rather than dismissed. This kind of empathetic engagement helps foster a sense of closure and respect. It shows that the court has not only ruled, but listened.

FOR WHOM DO WE WRITE?

Chief Justice of Canada Beverley McLachlin observed that key to communicating well through judgments is knowing the audience and knowing how the audience thinks.[66] When judges write, we do so not merely to resolve the dispute before us but also to speak to a constellation of audiences: the parties, the profession, the press, the public, and posterity.

The most immediate audience of a judgment is, of course, the *parties*. They are entitled to know why they have won or lost. Judicial reasoning that is impenetrable risks undermining the legitimacy of the decision it seeks to uphold. The parties must be able to see that their arguments were heard, their evidence considered, and their dignity respected. Even when the outcome is unfavourable, a well-reasoned judgment can affirm that the process was fair. It can soften the sting or disappointment of defeat by showing that the decision was not arbitrary and that the result was based on careful deliberation in accordance with the law. It can help parties come to terms with an unfavourable decision.[67]

Beyond the parties, we write for the *profession* – lawyers, judges, and the academy. Lawyers must advise clients, craft arguments, and anticipate how the law may evolve. They rely on judicial reasons (and particularly written reasons) not merely for the outcomes but also for their logic, structure, and interpretive signals. Judges – whether on appeal, reviewing decisions for legal and factual soundness, or at coordinate and subordinate levels, applying the law in future cases – look to judgments for clarity, coherence, and principled positions. The academy – academics and law students who study and critique the law – are also avid readers of judgments. Judgments enter the curriculum, shape commentary, and enrich the broader legal discourse. They serve as exemplars of legal reasoning, sources of doctrinal development, and, at times, catalysts for reform.

We write for the *press* – not only for the mainstream media, but for all forms of media that interpret and communicate judicial decisions to the public. From traditional newspapers and broadcast outlets to digital platforms, independent journalists, and legal commentators on social media. These intermediaries shape how the public understands the law and the role of the judiciary. A judgment that is clear, principled, and accessible helps ensure that this translation is accurate and constructive. In doing so, judicial writing contributes to informed public discourse and reinforces trust in the legal system.

We write for the *public* – the community we serve in the present. Judicial decisions are read, discussed, and relied upon by all who look to the courts for guidance, protection, and justice. Judgments are the judiciary's voice to society, expressing the values we uphold, the principles we apply, and the limits we observe. Our written reasons serve to foster public trust and affirm the rule of law.

And we write for *posterity* – future generations who will study our decisions to understand how judicial power was exercised and justified. Judgments become part of the legal and historical record, charting the evolution of doctrine and illuminating the way justice was served in society. In this way, our writing contributes to the long arc of legal development and to the collective understanding of how justice was dispensed over time.

Each of these audiences brings distinct expectations and interpretive lenses. At the risk of oversimplification: the parties seek fairness and recognition; the profession seeks doctrinal coherence and analytical rigour; the press seeks clarity and relevance to public discourse; and the public seeks reassurance that justice is principled and impartial. The sheer breadth of a judgment's audience renders this genre of writing 'more difficult than most other kinds'.[68] The surest way to reach such a diverse audience is to write judgments in plain, clear, and readily understood language – a task all the more challenging, yet all the more essential, when the case is complex.[69]

This multiplicity of audiences also underscores why written reasons matter. Oral explanations may suffice in some cases, but written judgments have the benefit of endurance. They can be archived, cited, studied, scrutinised, and critiqued. In this way, they shape not just the outcome of a single dispute but also the trajectory of the law itself.

HOW SHOULD WE WRITE?

Having considered *why* we write judgments and for *whom* we write, we now turn to the third inquiry: *how* should we write? This question does not stand apart from the earlier two. It arises *because* of them. Once we understand the purposes of judgment writing and the audiences to whom those purposes are owed, we can identify the values that must guide the craft. These values are the practical and ethical commitments that flow from a judge's responsibilities to the law and to the people affected by it. I suggest that there are at least four key values in the context of judgment writing.

First, *fidelity to law and fact*. Written reasons must demonstrate that judicial decisions are anchored in the legal framework and evidential record. This requires judges to engage with the parties' submissions, confront the legal issues squarely, and articulate the path from facts to conclusion. This commitment underlies the discussion in Chapter 2 (on writing robustly) and Chapter 3 (on structural discipline).

Second, *integrity of reasoning*. Writing is not merely a means of communication; it is a method of thought. The discipline of setting out one's reasons in writing tests the coherence of a decision and exposes weaknesses that may not be apparent in the abstract. A judgment that lacks internal integrity risks undermining the confidence of the various audiences identified earlier. This value is further explored in Chapter 2 (which emphasises the need for explanation and the avoidance of judicial plagiarism) and in Chapter 8 (which considers the responsibilities of authorship in an age of artificial intelligence).

Third, *respect for the law and for people*. Judges must communicate in a manner that is clear, structured, and accessible, so that the law can be understood, scrutinised, and applied. Suggestions for doing so are found in Chapter 3 (on structuring judgments tightly) and Chapter 4 (on writing precisely and concisely). Judges must also communicate respectfully and with humility, which is the focus of Chapter 5.

Fourth, *institutional stewardship*. Institutional stewardship requires that judges write with an awareness that each judgment is both an individual act and an institutional contribution. In this sense, every aspect of judgment writing has institutional significance, because each judgment shapes the public's perception of the judiciary as a whole. Chapter 7 adds a further dimension to this value by examining how, in a digital world, the form and presentation of judgments influence not only individual comprehension but also the accessibility, visibility, and authority of the court's institutional voice.

Of course, not all aspects of the judgment writing craft derive from these values alone. Some arise from the practical realities of judicial work. Chapter 6 therefore discusses techniques and methods that are not values in themselves, but which give effect to the values described earlier.

The values identified in this section do not operate in isolation. Together, they form the normative foundation for *how* we write. They are cross-cutting and do not map neatly onto individual chapters because each value informs several dimensions of the craft (as is evident from the prior multiple chapter references, which are themselves illustrative rather than exhaustive). While the chapters of this book are not grouped by values, these values are infused throughout, guiding the ways that judges can give effect to them when writing judgments.

CONCLUDING REFLECTIONS

Just as the 'black box' in aviation preserves the story of a flight – its trajectory, its turning points, its final moments – a well-reasoned judgment preserves the story of a legal dispute. It records not only what was decided but also how and why. It is a judge's way of saying: this decision was not arbitrary, it was reasoned; this decision was not merely imposed, it was justified (or, at the very least, explained).

In this chapter, we have explored *why* judges write, for *whom* we write, and *how* values should shape the way we write. We have seen that written judgments strengthen the rule of law, promote transparency and accountability, encourage accuracy, and affirm participation and respect. They are the means through which judges speak to the parties, the profession, the press, the public, and posterity. The rest of this book offers practical suggestions on how, guided by these foundational commitments, we might better express the voice of reason.

NOTES

1 Cherylann Mollan, 'India Recovers Data From Crashed Air India Flight Recorders' *BBC* (27 June 2025) <https://perma.cc/JP2J-YYVU>.

2 Mollan (n 1).

3 Stuart Jeffries, 'Secrets of the Black Box: How Does MH370's Flight Recorder Work?' *The Guardian* (31 March 2014) <https://perma.cc/65ZX-7CKR>.

4 'Black box' (*Cambridge Dictionary*) <https://perma.cc/2P43-R86C>.

5 Mathilde Cohen, 'When Judges Have Reasons Not to Give Reasons: A Comparative Law Approach' (2015) 72 Wash & Lee L Rev 483, 487.

6 'Pontificate' (*Merriam-Webster Dictionary*) <https://perma.cc/6U2V-QZGT>.

7 Cohen (n 5) 487.

8 Cohen (n 5) 488.
9 Cohen (n 5) 488.
10 Cohen (n 5) 558.
11 Cohen (n 5) 558.
12 Cohen (n 5) 559.
13 Cohen (n 5) 559, citing Michael Wells, 'French and American Judicial Opinions' (1994) 19 Yale J Intl L 81, 84.
14 Cohen (n 5) 559.
15 Cohen (n 5) 560.
16 'The History of the Commercial Court' (*Courts and Tribunals Judiciary*) <https://perma.cc/M9XV-J6HR>.
17 Lord Campbell, *The Lives of the Chief Justices of England*, vol 3 (James Cockcroft & Co 1874) 481, cited in *Thong Ah Fat v Public Prosecutor* [2011] SGCA 65, [2012] 1 SLR 676 [15].
18 Campbell (n 17) 481.
19 Chen Siyuan and Nicholas Poon, 'The Judicial Duty to Give Reasoned Decisions' (*Singapore Law Watch Commentary*, December 2011) <https://perma.cc/E9S4-3KLK>.
20 *Thong Ah Fat* (n 17) 15.
21 Ho Hock Lai, 'The Judicial Duty to Give Reasons' (2000) 20 Leg Stud 42, 43, citing examples from Australia, Canada, England, and New Zealand.
22 *Thong Ah Fat* (n 17) 15.
23 *Thong Ah Fat* (n 17) 32, citing *Sun Alliance Insurance Ltd v Massoud* [1989] VR 8 (Supreme Court of Victoria) 19.
24 *Thong Ah Fat* (n 17) 33, citing *Capital and Suburban Properties Ltd v Swycher* [1976] Ch 319 (CA) 325–326 and *Knight v Clifton* [1971] Ch 700 (CA) 721.
25 *Thong Ah Fat* (n 17) 33, citing *Eagil Trust Co Ltd v Pigott-Brown* [1985] 3 All ER 119 (CA) 122.
26 *Thong Ah Fat* (n 17) 46.
27 *Thong Ah Fat* (n 17) 31.
28 Ho (n 21) 48, citing *Coleman v Dunlop Ltd* (CA, 26 November 1997). See also *Thong Ah Fat* (n 17) 21.
29 Ho (n 21) 49, citing *Pettitt v Dunkley* [1971] 1 NSWLR 376 (NSWCA) 388. Note, however, that the absence of an avenue of appeal in itself does not mean that a court need not provide reasons – indeed, the absence of a right of appeal may make it 'all the more compelling for the parties to understand how it was reached': see *Thong Ah Fat* (n 17) 44.
30 As observed by the Singapore Court of Appeal, 'the legal profession and the community may ordinarily have legitimate interests in knowing these reasons. It enables practitioners, legislators and members of the public to ascertain the basis upon which like cases will probably be decided in the future': *Thong Ah Fat* (n 17) 21.
31 Lon Fuller, *The Morality of Law* (Rev edn, Yale University Press 1969) 46–91.
32 See e.g. *Beale v Government Insurance Office of NSW* (1997) 48 NSWLR 430 (NSWCA) 442, where the court observed, '[d]ecisions of courts usually influence the way in which society acts . . . it is better to understand why one should act [or not act] in a particular way.'
33 A term first introduced in Robert Mnookin and Lewis Kornhauser, 'Bargaining in the Shadow of the Law: The Case of Divorce' (1979) 88 Yale LJ 950.

34 See e.g. Mnookin and Kornhauser (n 33); Robert Cooter, Stephen Marks and Robert Mnookin, 'Bargaining in the Shadow of the Law: A Testable Model of Strategic Behavior' (1982) 11 J Leg Stud 225; and Stephanos Bibas, 'Plea Bargaining Outside the Shadow of Trial' (2004) 117 Harv L Rev 2463.

35 Cohen (n 5) 508.

36 Ho (n 21) 50.

37 As a matter of trivia, Judge Learned Hand's full name was 'Billings Learned Hand'. However, he dropped the word 'Billings' (taking on the nickname 'B') as he found it 'pompous'. See Marvin Schick, *Learned Hand's Court* (Johns Hopkins Press 1970) 13.

38 See Chapter 8, and the 'Learned Hand Judicial Case Preparation Platform' at <http://www.learned-hand.ai> accessed 5 May 2026 (with a permanent link captured at <https://perma.cc/RE6F-6CY5>).

39 Ross Guberman, *Point Taken: How to Write Like the World's Best Judges* (Oxford University Press 2015) xxii.

40 Guberman (n 39) xxii.

41 Beverley McLachlin, 'Judicial Accountability' (Speech at the Conference on Law and Parliament, Ottawa, 2 November 2006) <https://perma.cc/5XHR-7QMB>.

42 This is the case in many judicial codes of conduct worldwide, including Singapore's. Justice William Brennan of the United States Supreme Court explained in 1959 that 'the reasons behind the social policy fostering an independent judiciary also require that the opinions by which judges support decisions must stand on their own merits without embellishment or comment from the judges who write or join them': Alan F Westin, 'Out-of-Court Commentary by United States Supreme Court Justices, 1790–1962: Of Free Speech and Judicial Lockjaw' (1962) 62(4) Col L Rev 633.

43 Cohen (n 5) 501.

44 Cohen (n 5) 501, 502.

45 Cohen (n 5) 499.

46 Michael Serota, 'Intelligible Justice' (2012) 66 U Miami L Rev 649, 654.

47 Serota (n 46) 649, citing Ray Forrester, 'Supreme Court Opinions – Style and Substance: An Appeal for Reform' (1995) 47 Hastings LJ 167, 173.

48 Cohen (n 5) 511

49 *Thong Ah Fat* (n 17) 22.

50 See e.g. Ronald Dworkin, *Freedom's Law: The Moral Reading of the American Constitution* (Harvard University Press 1997) 345.

51 I discuss this more in Chapter 8.

52 *Beale* (n 32) 442.

53 Richard Posner, 'Judges' Writing Styles (And Do They Matter?)' (1995) 62 U Chi L Rev 1421, 1447.

54 *Thong Ah Fat* (n 17) 20; Doron Menashe, 'The Requirement of Reasons for Findings of Fact' (2006) Intl C L Rev 223, 230.

55 Gerald Lebovits, Alifya Curtin, and Lisa Solomon, 'Ethical Judicial Opinion Writing' (2008) 21 Geo J Legal Ethics 237.

56 The Rt Hon Sir Harry Gibbs, 'Judgment Writing' (February 1994) The Arbitrator 197, 198–199 <https://perma.cc/R5H5-9NMH>, citing Sir Frank Kitto, 'Why Write Judgments?' (Address at the Judges' Conference, Hobart, 1973), subsequently published at (1992) 66 ALJ 787.

57 Ho (n 21) 49, citing various sources such as RN Komar, *Reasons for Judgment* (Butterworths 1980) 9.

58 Serota (n 46) 653.

59 See e.g. Daniel Kahneman, *Thinking, Fast and Slow* (Farrar, Straus and Giroux 2011); Zhuang Liu, 'Does Reason Writing Reduce Decision Bias? Experimental Evidence From Judges in China' (2018) 47 J Leg Stud 83.

60 Cohen (n 5) 508.

61 Cohen (n 5) 505.

62 Lon Fuller, 'Forms and Limits of Adjudication' (1978) 92 Harv L Rev 353, 388.

63 Ho (n 21) 4950.

64 *Connell v Auckland City Council* [1977] 1 NZLR 630 (NZHC) 634 (Chilwell J).

65 RE Megarry, *Lawyer and Litigant in England* (Stevens & Sons Limited 1962) 135.

66 Beverley McLachlin (Remarks at the NJI and CIAJ Advanced Judgment Writing Seminar, Perth, 16 May 2010) <https://perma.cc/MN5T-358F> 10.

67 Ho (n 21) 50, observing, 'the withholding of reasons may affect the *acceptability* of the decision' (emphasis in original).

68 Edward Berry, *Writing Reasons: A Handbook for Judges* (5th edn, LexisNexis Canada 2020) xii.

69 McLachlin (n 66) 11.

Writing That Persuades – Writing Robustly

Two

Sherlock Holmes – arguably the best-known detective of all time – has long been one of my favourite characters. In one of his most well-loved adventures, *The Speckled Band*, an extract of Holmes' concluding explanation to his associate Dr John Watson (and to the reader) included the following:[1]

> *An inspection of his chair showed me that he had been in the habit of standing on it, which of course would be necessary in order that he should reach the ventilator. The sight of the safe, the saucer of milk and the loop of whipcord were enough finally to dispel any doubts which may have remained. The metallic clang heard by Miss Stoner was obviously caused by her stepfather hastily closing the door of his safe upon its terrible occupant. Having once made up my mind, you know the steps which I took in order to put the matter to the proof. I heard the creature hiss, as I have no doubt that you did also, and I instantly lit the light and attacked it.*

This extract is a brief but characteristic demonstration of Holmes' technique of robust reasoning. It is often said that his deductions are carefully built, with each proposition supported by clues that may have appeared insignificant to everyone else. Strictly speaking, Holmes' method is *abductive*, not deductive: he arrives at his conclusion by inferring the most plausible explanation for a state of affairs, rather than deriving truth through syllogisms.[2] But no matter the technical epistemological label for Holmes' method, the essence of his technique is simple: he shows his workings, rather than simply asserts 'because I say so'. That, more than his eloquence or the flourish of his final reveal, is what makes his pronouncements truly persuasive.

Like Holmes, a judge must justify conclusions – not assume them – lest reason give way to mere rhetoric. Authority may grant a judge the power to decide, but only robust reasoned explanation will persuade the reader that the decision rests on law and logic. This is foundational to earning the trust of not just those affected by the judgment but also of the public. Such trust must be earned, one judgment at a time.

DOI: 10.4324/9781042017027-3

Some may question if the reference to persuasion is appropriate. After all, is persuasion not a task for the advocate rather than the judge? Not quite. Not if we understand persuasion to mean the force of effective reasoned argument. As Professor Edward Berry has suggested, persuasion in this sense is quite different from the connotations that link it with 'slick rhetoric' and 'sly deceptions'.[3] Rather, it refers to the force of effective legal reasoning that explains the decision. The art of persuasion is important in judgment writing 'not because it clouds reason but because it clarifies it'.[4]

This chapter explores what it means to persuade through robust writing. It begins with the need for explanation – a nod to the Holmesian approach of persuading by revealing the reasoning, not merely the result. It then turns to the discipline of engaging with parties' positions (especially the losing party's) as a safeguard against error and a gesture of respect. From there, it highlights the need for block quotations to be framed, distilled, and explained to aid reader comprehension. Finally, the chapter confronts the issue of judicial plagiarism, reminding us that robust writing is very much about earning trust by speaking with the court's own voice of reason.

THE NEED FOR EXPLANATION

A conclusion must be explained, not merely stated. The Singapore Court of Appeal could not have expressed itself more clearly on this point when in *Thong Ah Fat v Public Prosecutor* it emphasised:[5]

> *A legal judgment today cannot be justified solely by the judge's statement of belief that it is right, without providing any explanation as to why it is so. The days when it sufficed for a judge to say 'Because I say so' are well behind us. The legal cogency and coherence of a decision must therefore also be demonstrated to justify it.*

The court also urged that a judgment should 'examine the relevant evidence and the facts found with a view to explaining the final outcome on each material issue'.[6]

There are various contexts in which explanation is required in a judgment. Take, for instance, the context of credibility assessment – a domain where the need for explanation is especially acute, and which was considered in detail in *Thong Ah Fat*. The court emphasised the importance of judges explicating how they arrived at their conclusions on credibility, observing that '[i]mpressionistic statements are not helpful'.[7] It cautioned against the 'questionable' practice of relying formulaically on demeanour, without more, to justify a finding of credibility.[8] That caution is well supported by research that casts doubt on the reliability of demeanour as a proxy for truthfulness: judges are often no better than chance at detecting deception based on body language or tone alone.[9] People vary widely in their expressive behaviour, which can lead a decision-maker to disbelieve the truth and believe a falsehood.[10] All this underscores the importance of anchoring credibility assessments in objective evidence wherever possible.

One example can be drawn from *Thong Ah Fat* itself. The judge below described the evidence given by the accused as 'very thin'.[11] The court observed that this did not shed any light on whether the accused person's evidence was disbelieved because of his demeanour when giving oral testimony in court, because its content was inconsistent with extrinsic objective evidence, or for some other reason. There was no analysis of the supposedly 'very thin' evidence, which the court found to be unsatisfactory because it was unclear whether the judge below had considered objective evidence which supported the accused person's contentions.

Of course, a judge may sometimes have little option but to decide based on 'overall impression rather than by methodical reasoning'.[12] This happens, for instance, when there are contradictory accounts between witnesses, with no other supporting evidence on either side, leaving the entire decision to turn on which witness the court believes. However, it is a 'rare case' where there is such a complete absence of objective evidence that the decision turns entirely on the evidence of a single witness.[13]

The same discipline that is required in credibility findings applies equally to the rest of a judgment. Explanation must do the work; rhetoric cannot. It is sometimes tempting to reach for rhetorical shortcuts – such as formulaic dismissals or stock phrases – and assume that they suffice as explanation. Expressions such as 'with respect, this submission is untenable' or 'this argument is wholly without merit' sound judicial indeed. However, they risk substituting tone for thought and masking the absence of real analysis. A party's submission may be flawed, but unless the judge explains how and why it is so, the reader is left with assertion rather than persuasion. Far better, then, for the judge to engage with the substance of the argument, identify its weaknesses, and explain the basis for disagreeing with it.

The following contrasting examples, taken from a hypothetical dispute under a licensing statute that requires ministerial approval in certain circumstances, illustrate the point. First, an example deploying the use of rhetorical shortcuts:

> *With respect, the Defendant's interpretation of section 12(3) of the Licensing Act cannot be accepted. The court has considered the submissions carefully and is unable to agree with the construction advanced. The provision, read in its proper context, does not support the Defendant's position. The Defendant's argument therefore fails.*

Contrast this with a version with more robust analysis:

> *The Defendant argued that section 12(3) of the Licensing Act permits it to operate additional outlets without prior approval, on the basis that the phrase 'subject to the conditions prescribed' refers only to administrative requirements. This interpretation cannot be accepted. When section 12(3) is read together with section 12(4), it becomes evident that any expansion of operations that substantially increases the scale of the licensed activity requires prior ministerial approval. The Defendant's proposed expansion falls squarely within that category, and no approval was obtained. The Defendant's argument therefore fails.*

ADDRESSING PARTIES' POSITIONS

Robust writing requires engagement with the parties' positions – not simply as a procedural gesture but also as a substantive discipline. This means neither repeating submissions at length nor addressing every minor point. Rather, it means responding to the essence of what was argued and ensuring that there are clear decisions taken on the central issues.[14] This may sometimes require the court to synthesise, restate, or reorganise the parties' arguments.[15] The purpose is not to substitute its own formulation but to present the parties' arguments in their strongest and most coherent form. Ultimately, parties deserve to know that their main arguments were taken seriously, understood, and tested.[16]

This is particularly important in relation to the losing party. In a case where the court below had largely engaged only with the winning party's arguments, Chief Justice of Singapore Sundaresh Menon urged judges to 'note the particular importance of directing the reasons behind their decision to the losing party'.[17]

Addressing the losing party's arguments is critical to helping the losing party to understand *why* they lost and providing assurance that the result was in accordance with the law. Engaging with the unsuccessful party's arguments also provides an important guardrail against error in reasoning. Chief Justice Beverley McLachlin observed extra-judicially that the greatest assurance to the public is when a judgment 'frankly and fully' addresses the losing party's arguments.[18] It is, she said, 'perhaps the greatest check against an incorrect conclusion'.[19] After all, when a judge can explain why an opposing argument fails, it is a strong indication that the issues have been fully understood, thus strengthening the reasoning and judiciousness of the decision. Conversely, if a judge cannot explain the argument's failure, it may suggest that the issues have not been completely grasped.

The upshot of the aforementioned is that a judgment should address the parties' positions,[20] and that it is especially critical to expressly engage the losing party's position.

As a matter of judgment structure, there are two main ways to address the parties' positions. The preferred approach depends on the circumstances of the point being discussed.

The Dialectic Approach

The first is the 'dialectic approach', which proceeds along these lines:

> *Party A says X. Party B says Y. The Court says X (or Z).*

This approach needs little elaboration. It is commonly deployed because it is intuitive and straightforward, especially in the context of adversarial systems where a judge arrives at a decision after hearing the arguments on both sides.

The LOPP/FLOPP Approach

There is a second approach which involves – to borrow Professor James Raymond's terminology[21] – addressing the 'Losing Party's Position' and 'Flaw in the Losing Party's Position' (referred to in shorthand as the 'LOPP/FLOPP approach'). The structure is as follows:

> *Party B says Y. But the Court says X because . . .*

This approach provides relative economy because the winning party's position is not canvassed at any length. For that reason, this structure works well only when the court's decision is based on its agreement with the position advanced by the winning party. Where the court has decided for reasons other than those advanced by the winning party, the dialectic approach is more appropriate so that the parties and the reader can understand why the court declined to adopt either party's position.

In relation to the LOPP stage, in stating the argument of the losing party (i.e., Party B in the prior examples), the judge must endeavour to state the argument as clearly and charitably as possible. Indeed, it may sometimes be useful for the judge to clarify or refine Party B's argument, rather than to proceed only on Party B's original formulation, which may be convoluted or imprecise. Doing so ensures that the court engages with the strongest version of the argument rather than with a straw man. Thereafter, at the FLOPP stage, the judge should identify as clearly as possible the flaw in the losing party's position. The ability to do so demonstrates that the judge has understood the losing party's argument and can test whether it holds.

The main benefit of the LOPP/FLOPP approach is its economy. Foregrounding the position of the losing party is an 'easy way' to shorten the discussion on the parties' positions,[22] thus reducing the exposition required by the judgment writer, and the volume of reading required by the reader. That said, three caveats are worth noting.

First, as mentioned earlier, the LOPP/FLOPP approach works well only when the court agrees with the winning party's position. If the court finds for the winning party for reasons different from those raised by the winning party, the failure to address the winning party's arguments (and to explain why the court disagreed with them) would result in the winning party being uncertain as to whether the court understood and considered its arguments.

Second, in cases where the (eventually successful) party must first establish a *prima facie* case before any evidential burden shifts to the other (eventually unsuccessful) party, there is a risk that excessive focus on the weaknesses of the unsuccessful party's case may obscure the prior and more fundamental inquiry: whether the successful party had in fact met that initial threshold.[23]

Third, there are contexts in which identifying a 'losing party' may be inappropriate or unhelpful. Professor James Raymond has observed that family matters involving child custody provide one such context, as it is often helpful to avoid framing outcomes in terms of a winning or losing party.[24] Instead, the judgment can be structured around key considerations – such as proximity to schools, access to extended family, and the child's safety – with each factor used to compare and contrast the parents' respective household circumstances. Even where the decision ultimately turns on the unsuitability of one parent, it remains valuable to acknowledge that parent's strengths alongside the shortcomings that led to the court's conclusion.[25] Doing so affirms participation and respect for the parties.

Ultimately, regardless of the approach chosen (i.e., whether dialectic or LOPP/FLOPP), the goal remains the same: to demonstrate that the court has understood the parties' positions, tested them, and arrived at a reasoned conclusion.

DIGESTING, NOT DUMPING

Judgments sometimes reproduce long block quotes from precedents, legislation, academic commentary, or hearing transcripts. This may be necessary when the precise wording is critical to the case at hand. But quotations, particularly long block quotes, should not be unthinkingly used. A formidable wall of block-quoted words may add an appearance of robustness, but the reality is that readers often jump right over the wall once it is in sight. The longer the block quote, the more likely it is to be ignored, especially if it is not properly framed, digested, or explained.

Professor Edward Berry reminds us:[26]

> *Block quotations also add unnecessary length to judgments – of statutes, precedents, testimony, decisions of a lower court, and more. In writing programs, judges are often asked what they do as readers when they come to a block quotation on a page. The invariable response? 'Skip it.' What is it about a mere indentation on a page that can make the eyes glaze over, the mind fidget, and the finger move restlessly to the next page? I suspect it is a conditioned reflex, a healthy Pavlovian response to habitual experience: if I read this, we think, I am bound to be bored and more likely to be confused than enlightened. Conciseness is not the only virtue sacrificed by quotation of this kind; clarity usually accompanies her to the altar.*

Did you read Professor Berry's block quote more carefully than the paragraphs before it? Did you read the block quote *at all*? If your answer to either question is 'no', that is precisely the point. A block quote, however vivid or well written, often becomes a visual and cognitive obstacle. Its very formatting signals to the reader: 'Here is something to be endured, not engaged with'. The quotation may be authoritative and elegant. But unless it is framed and digested by the present writer, it risks being skipped over. The reader's attention is sometimes lost, not by the content of the quote, but by the sheer fact of its indentation.

With the digital tools we have today, the temptation to block quote is strong. All it takes is a few keystrokes – 'Ctrl+C' / 'Ctrl+V' (or 'Cmd+C' / 'Cmd+V') – and pristine chunks of text appear on the page. This may be useful in early drafts where effort is arguably better spent thinking through the substance of the points made rather than their eventual presentation, but one should not unthinkingly allow block quotes to remain in the final version. Instead, as part of reviewing a draft judgment, one should pause at each block quote and consider whether one is digesting or dumping. A useful question to ask is: 'Would this block quote be more impactful if paraphrased?'

If the answer is 'yes', then there is little reason to retain the block quote. It is, of course, possible that the answer is 'no, a block quote is preferable'. This may be because the block quote has specific explanatory force that will be lost through a paraphrase, or because it constitutes the precise evidence at issue (such as where the block quote reproduces something that a witness said, or a material clause in a contract).

If the decision is that a block quote is required, it is useful to consider three further points in the interest of aiding a reader's digestion of the material.

First, whether a shorter extract might be sufficient.[27] A shorter block quote is easier to read than a long one, and therefore less likely to be skipped over by a reader.

Second, if the full extract is required for context, whether any key parts of the quote should be emphasised by *italicised*, **bold**, or ***bold italicised*** text.

Third, whether explanatory context should be provided prior to introducing the quote, so that the reader is primed to focus on what really matters when the wall of words arrives.[28] It is usually better to state upfront the reason for quoting the passage ('In *ABC v XYZ*, the court identified three factors relevant to assessing intentionality') rather than to rely on a perfunctory introduction ('In *ABC v XYZ*, the court held as follows'). This signals to the reader what to look for and why the quote is being included. The framing acts as a guidepost, helping the reader navigate the quoted material rather than wade through it in search of its significance.

AVOIDING JUDICIAL PLAGIARISM

The discussion on block quotes segues neatly into this final section on judicial plagiarism. Judgment writing must reflect the genuine thinking of its author. Copying passages wholesale can undermine this, regardless of whether the source of copying is a party's submissions, another authority, or even a previous judgment of one's own.

Plagiarism in this context is more than just intellectual theft. It is also about intellectual disengagement. A judgment that cuts and pastes another's analysis without explanation creates the impression that the judge may not have reasoned independently. It raises questions about whether the judge has really applied an independent mind to the facts and arguments at hand, and whether the judge made the decision under the sway of bias.

The Singapore courts have eschewed judicial plagiarism in the strongest possible terms. In *Yap Ah Lai*[29] and *Newton David Christopher*,[30] the courts emphasised that the wholesale adoption of a party's submissions or passages from other cases (including the judge's own prior decisions) may offer reasonable basis for concluding that the judge did not fully appreciate or apply an independent mind to the facts, arguments, issues, and circumstances in the case before the court, and that the judge had failed to decide impartially and independently. Similarly, in *Lim Chee Huat*,[31] the court suggested that copying submissions may raise the concern that the judge is (or appears to be) biased in favour of the party whose submissions were copied. Such copying may suggest that the judgment is 'not merely an error of the exercise of judgment but a judgment in name only that was not the exercise of any consideration and weighing'.[32]

In *Ler Chun Poh*,[33] even paraphrased borrowing was found problematic when used without explanation, because it cast doubt on whether the judge had truly calibrated the reasoning to the case at hand. The court observed that while the judge below did address mitigating and aggravating factors on the facts of the case before him, the extensive borrowing from a previous case 'robbed that part of his Grounds of Decision of any characteristic of proper analysis'.[34]

There will, of course, be times when a prior decision contains phrasing so apt that it deserves quotation. This is acceptable so long as it is acknowledged and contextualised to the case at hand. Subject to what has been discussed in the earlier section titled 'Digesting, Not Dumping', quoting a well-crafted passage can reinforce the reasoning or link the current decision to an established line of authority.

A judgment must reflect the judge's own engagement with the matter before the court. Borrowed language may support the court's reasoning, but must not substitute for it. When large swathes of a judgment – be they factual summaries, legal principles, or analysis – are lifted wholesale from earlier judgments or parties' submissions, the result is a kind of judicial ventriloquism: the court speaks, but its voice is not entirely its own.

CONCLUDING REFLECTIONS

Holmes persuaded not just by theatrical flourish, but (more importantly) by the transparency and cogency of his reasoning. That same discipline underpins robust judicial writing. Such writing explains, engages, and resists the temptation to borrow excessively from others. In doing so, the court affirms its role not merely as a decider of disputes but also as a steward of public trust – a role it fulfils not by authority alone, but through the discipline of robust, reasoned writing.

NOTES

1 Sir Arthur Conan Doyle, *The Best of Sherlock Holmes* (Macmillan Collector's Library 2016) 225, 226.

2 Justin Yeo, 'Of Epistemology, Ethics and Evidential Rules in Evidence Law' (2010) <https://perma.cc/72NR-HUPQ>.

3 Edward Berry, *Writing Reasons: A Handbook for Judges* (6th edn, LexisNexis Canada 2025) xi.

4 Berry (n 3) xi.

5 *Thong Ah Fat v Public Prosecutor* [2011] SGCA 65, [2012] 1 SLR 676 [17].

6 *Thong Ah Fat* (n 5) 36.

7 *Thong Ah Fat* (n 5) 37.

8 *Thong Ah Fat* (n 5) 38.

9 Maureen O'Sullivan and Paul Ekman, 'The Wizards of Deception Detection' in PA Granhag and LA Strömwall (eds), *The Detection of Deception in Forensic Contexts* (Cambridge University Press 2009) 269.

10 Hazel Genn, 'Assessing Credibility' (*Courts and Tribunals Judiciary*, 20 January 2016) <https://perma.cc/ACL3-A4KV>.

11 *Public Prosecutor v Thong Ah Fat* [2010] SGHC 227 [4].

12 *Thong Ah Fat* (n 5) 37.

13 *Thong Ah Fat* (n 5) 38.

14 *Thong Ah Fat* (n 5) 36.

15 As an example, see *Gillingham James Ian v Fearless Legends Pte Ltd* [2023] SGHCR 13 [8] to [10], where the court synthesised the respondents' multiple arguments under nine different headings. Note that the reported version of the judgment ([2024] 6 SLR 697) is limited only to selected issues and does not include the court's synthesis of arguments. This case is also mentioned in Chapter 4, text accompanying n 26.

16 See the discussion on the importance of participation of the parties in Chapter 1 ('Affirming Participation and Respect').

17 *Newton David Christopher v Public Prosecutor* [2023] SGHC 266, [2024] 3 SLR 1370 [40(c)].

18 Beverley McLachlin (Remarks at the NJI and CIAJ Advanced Judgment Writing Seminar, Perth, 16 May 2010) <https://perma.cc/MN5T-358F> 9.

19 McLachlin (n 18) 9.

20 *Thong Ah Fat* (n 5) 35.

21 James Raymond, 'The Architecture of Argument' (2004) 7 The Judicial Review: J Jud Comm New South Wales 39, 44.

22 Berry (n 3) 53.

23 For instance, in *Mak-Levrion Kah Kay Natasha v R Shiamala* [2023] SGHC 335, [2024] 4 SLR 616, the Singapore High Court found that while the assistant registrar had granted summary judgment on the basis that the defendant had failed to raise a suitable defence, the claimant had not in fact discharged her burden of establishing a *prima facie* case in the first place.

24 Raymond (n 21) 45.

25 Raymond (n 21) 45. See also the discussion in Chapter 1 (on 'Affirming Participation and Respect').

26 Berry (n 3) 51.

27 Berry (n 3) 51.

28 Berry (n 3) 65–68.

29 *Yap Ah Lai v Public Prosecutor* [2014] SGHC 70, [2014] 3 SLR 180 [69].

30 *Newton David Christopher* (n 17) 40(a).

31 *Lim Chee Huat v Public Prosecutor* [2019] SGHC 132, [2019] 5 SLR 433 [49].

32 *Lim Chee Huat* (n 32) 52.

33 *Ler Chun Poh v Public Prosecutor* [2024] SGHC 307, [2024] 6 SLR 410 [27].

34 *Ler Chun Poh* (n 33) 46.

From Chaos to Clarity – Writing Tightly

Three

There was a time when my son's room was a monument to curiosity: puzzle pieces nestled in toy trucks, musical instruments tossed amongst Lego blocks and dried-out Play-Doh, and books scattered around in defiance of the shelves we provided. Despite our best efforts in cajoling and packing, his treasures remained gloriously strewn across every available surface. He got away with it most of the time – for toddlers are (usually) permitted a kind of joyful chaos.

Judgment writers are offered no such indulgence. A judgment cannot have its facts, law, submissions, analysis, and findings scattered haphazardly across its pages. One empathises that, having expended significant time and energy on reasoning, a judge may have little appetite left for the labour of tidying and structuring. But unless the judge invests effort in ordering the room, readers are left to fend for themselves.

Marie Kondo taught that tidying is not about minimalism as a value in itself, but about intentionality – deciding what to keep, what to discard, and how to arrange what remains so that it serves the purpose of the person who lives with it. Her method is about ensuring that everything has its place, and nothing is there without purpose. To her, it is critical to identify what 'sparks joy', and to let go of the rest.[1] While maintaining the perfect state of tidiness is less of a priority for her now – perhaps unsurprisingly because of the demands of parenthood that leave 'kids' toys . . . strewn across her formerly immaculate home'[2] – the deeper lesson on intentionality endures.

Judgments may not spark joy in a traditional sense, save perhaps for the successful party or the judge signing off on the final version (with a sigh of relief). But there is joy in a judgment that is well structured, navigable, and intelligible.

This chapter explores how keeping writing tight through structural strategies can help enhance the clarity of written judgments. It begins with the discipline of structure – how the overall organisation of a judgment, especially when sorted by issue, can enhance

DOI: 10.4324/9781042017027-4

readability and persuasion. It then turns to the role of headings as signposts for both writer and reader, before considering the value of starting with the conclusion as a way of guiding the journey. Finally, it confronts the temptation to include everything and offers strategies for resisting the 'kitchen sink' approach.

Ultimately, judgment writing is not simply about wordsmithing or putting ideas into words. It is also a *structural* endeavour: how do we arrange the contents of our writing so that someone else can walk into the room and understand where to find what?

DESIGNING THE FRAMEWORK: JUDGMENT STRUCTURE

The way a judgment is organised shapes how tight it is – how its facts are absorbed, how its arguments unfold, and how its conclusions are understood. While certain structural habits have long been adopted in judgment writing, they can and should be reconsidered. This section explores three broad approaches to structuring a judgment – 'Fact-Driven', 'Issue-Driven', and 'Hybrid' – and considers how each affects the reader's experience and the writer's discipline.

Fact-Driven Approach

Traditional judicial writing often proceeds in a structure that has been called the Fact-Driven approach.[3] A schematic representation of this approach is as follows:

- **INTRODUCTION**
- **FACTS**
  (*usually chronologically set out*)
- **LAW**
- **DISCUSSION / ANALYSIS**
- **CONCLUSION**

This approach is perhaps the most convenient for a judgment writer. It mirrors the natural process of judicial reasoning. Judges often work through the factual matrix before crystallising the legal issues that arise. It also mimics the sequence of the proceedings, where parties adduce evidence before putting forward submissions on the law and its application to the facts.

But for the reader, the Fact-Driven approach poses two main challenges.

First, lengthy sections containing background facts or law may be presented without immediate indication of how they are relevant to the decision. When perusing these sections, the reader is left holding multiple thoughts in suspense, unsure which matter and why. When the application of the law to the facts finally arrives, the reader may struggle to recall earlier details or understand how they connect. The reader may press on with a vague recollection of what had been discussed earlier, or flip back and forth through the judgment to refresh that memory. Some judges try to help by cross-referencing specific paragraphs in the earlier sections, but this does not save the reader from having to jump around the judgment in order to follow the judge's reasoning.

Second, some judges address the problem by restating the facts or law relevant to each issue when discussing the issue. This unfortunately results in repetition.[4] Facts are first laid out in the 'Background Facts' section, legal principles in the 'Law' section, and both are revisited in the 'Discussion' or 'Analysis' section. The result is a lengthier judgment that, again, tests the reader's patience and increases the cognitive load required for understanding the judgment.

Both challenges increase the reader's cognitive load, and the force of the judgment may be diluted by the effort required to follow it.

Issue-Driven Approach

An alternative to the Fact-Driven approach is the Issue-Driven approach. This Issue-Driven approach organises a judgment around the issues for determination, or any other discrete component (such as individual charges or specific heads of claim) that the court must resolve. The discussions of each issue (i.e., the facts relevant to each issue, the law relevant to each issue, the application of the law to facts, and the decision on each issue) take place as standalone sections. In its 'pure' form, the judgment may come to resemble several 'mini judgments'. A schematic representation of this approach is as follows:

- **INTRODUCTION**
- **OVERVIEW OF ISSUES**
- **ISSUE 1**
  - **FACTS** (relevant to Issue 1)
  - **PARTIES' POSITIONS** (on Issue 1)

- **LAW** *(relevant to issue 1)*
- **DISCUSSION / ANALYSIS** *(on Issue 1)*
- **CONCLUSION** *(on Issue 1)*

- **ISSUE 2**
  - **FACTS** *(relevant to Issue 2)*
  - **PARTIES' POSITIONS** *(on Issue 2)*
  - **LAW** *(relevant to Issue 2)*
  - **DISCUSSION / ANALYSIS** *(on Issue 2)*
  - **CONCLUSION** *(on Issue 2)*
- . . . *(Repeat as required for each issue)*
- **CONCLUSION**

An example of a 'pure' Issue-Driven approach is found in *Public Prosecutor v Henry Koh Yik Wee*,[5] where the court dealt with each of the two criminal charges in its own self-contained section, complete with separate discussions of the facts and analysis. Each section was sufficiently discrete that it could almost be read as a standalone judgment.

One major benefit of the Issue-Driven approach is that it sets out the discussion of the facts and law in the context of the issues to which they relate – that is, it gives effect to the principle of proximity.[6] The Issue-Driven approach enhances the structural tightness of a judgment by allowing readers to engage with one issue at a time, without carrying the entire weight of the case in their minds. The Issue-Driven approach also enhances readability, because proximity obviates the need for tedious cross-referencing and may also help minimise repetition within the judgment.

The Issue-Driven approach offers significant benefits in terms of clarity and reader guidance. However, it has its own challenges, two of which I discuss here.

First, the Issue-Driven approach often requires more effort from the judgment writer. It requires the writer to tidy the room by organising the facts and law, issue by issue. This calls for considerable discipline and iterative redrafting, because the natural rhythm of judicial reasoning may well follow the model of the Fact-Driven approach: judges often work through the entire factual matrix before crystallising the legal issues that arise. Structuring the judgment by issue, therefore, may feel counter-intuitive to the judgment writer's thought process. This additional layer of categorisation demands a higher degree of analytical effort and editorial discipline. It also requires the writer to anticipate the structure of the Judgment early on, which may be difficult in cases where the issues evolve over the course of writing.

Second, there are cases – especially complex cases – where the issues are not easily separable, where facts and law are interwoven across multiple issues, or where the application and analysis depend on a holistic view of the facts. Forcing such a judgment into an issue-by-issue segmented structure may obscure the interconnectedness of the reasoning or lead to repetition when the same facts must be revisited in multiple sections.

Hybrid Approach

The third possibility is a Hybrid approach.[7] The Hybrid approach is useful in situations where there is scope for issue-by-issue analysis, but where a full Issue-Driven structure may be too rigid, time-consuming, or repetitive. It is particularly useful in cases with a complex factual background but relatively discrete legal issues, or where the chronology itself is central to understanding the dispute.

A common manifestation of the Hybrid approach sees an initial section setting out the general background facts to serve a narrative function (usually, chronologically). This situates the dispute in time and context, offering a coherent storyline that anchors the judgment. The Hybrid approach then reserves the more detailed and contested facts for discussion under each identified issue. These additional facts are introduced in the context of the specific legal issues to which they relate, thus enhancing the proximity between fact, law, and analysis. A schematic representation of this approach is as follows:

- **INTRODUCTION**
- **BACKGROUND FACTS**
  (*only a brief narrative background; this may be chronologically set out to help situate the dispute in time and context*)
- **OVERVIEW OF ISSUES**
- **ISSUE 1**
  - **FACTS** (*relevant to Issue 1*)
  - **PARTIES' POSITIONS** (*on Issue 1*)

- **LAW** (*relevant to Issue 1*)
- **DISCUSSION / ANALYSIS** (*on Issue 1*)
- **CONCLUSION** (*on Issue 1*)

- **ISSUE 2**
  - **FACTS** (*relevant to Issue 2*)
  - **PARTIES' POSITIONS** (*on Issue 2*)
  - **LAW** (*relevant to Issue 2*)
  - **DISCUSSION / ANALYSIS** (*on Issue 2*)
  - **CONCLUSION** (*on Issue 2*)
- . . . (*Repeat as required for each issue*)
- **CONCLUSION**

This structure combines the intuitive flow of the traditional Fact-Driven approach with the clarity and coherence of the Issue-Driven approach.

This Hybrid approach has been adopted in various Singapore judgments. See, for instance, *Public Prosecutor v Ridhaudin Ridhwan bin Bakri*.[8] In this case, the 'Background' section offered a narrative overview of the facts to provide context (i.e., the Fact-Driven approach), providing a chronological account of the series of sexual assaults against the victim by the various defendants, at various times, and at various locations. This chronological narrative then formed a scaffold for the analysis that follows in the section on 'My Decision on the Charges', which is structured charge by charge, with detailed facts relating to each instance of assault set out in the subsection discussing each charge. Another example is *Eugene Phoa v Oey Liang Ho*,[9] which I discuss further in the later section relating to headings.

There is no one-size-fits-all solution to a judgment's structure.[10] The choice of the judgment's structure should ultimately be guided by the nature of the case and the needs of the reader.

SETTING THE SCENE: CRAFTING ENGAGING INTRODUCTIONS

Every judgment has an introduction. However, not every introduction serves its function of setting the scene and engaging the reader. The introduction is the judge's first opportunity to frame the dispute, establish the tone, and prepare the reader for the journey ahead. A good introduction draws the reader in and assures the reader that the judgment is worthy of the reader's time.

Judgment introductions tend to fall along a spectrum. At one end lies what Professor Edward Berry calls the 'bureaucratic introduction': an introduction that carries an 'apparent indifference to the human side of the judgment', as well as to 'compress as much technical information as possible into the first paragraph'.[11] An example of such an introduction, generated by generative artificial intelligence ('GenAI') based on one of my published judgments, reads as follows:

> This matter concerns the sentencing of Mr [. . .] ('the *Accused*'), a [. . .]-year-old Singaporean male, arising from events that occurred between approximately [time] on [date] and [time] on [date] at a place that cannot be disclosed due to a gag order made on [date]. The *Accused* pleaded guilty to a charge under s [. . .] of the Penal Code, which reads as follows:
>
> [Charge set out in full]
>
> The present proceedings arise from an agreed Statement of Facts dated [date] and follow the Prosecution's submission for a custodial sentence of [. . .] to [. . .] months' imprisonment together with [. . .] strokes of the cane, and the Defence's submission for an imprisonment term of [. . .] months. Following a hearing on [date], and having considered the parties' respective positions, the applicable statutory framework, and the relevant sentencing principles, the court imposes a sentence of [. . .] months' imprisonment and [. . .] strokes of the cane. The factual background, procedural history, and reasons for sentence are set out below for completeness and ease of reference.

At the other end of the spectrum lies the 'writerly introduction', which is 'designed to call attention to itself'.[12] An example of such an introduction, again generated by GenAI based on the same published judgment, reads as follows:[13]

> In this case, we are confronted with a sobering tale. What began as a meandering night of idle pleasures soon unfurled into a grim parable of human frailty and human choice.
>
> Two men, finding before them two women rendered defenceless by drink, stood at a crossroads familiar to the conscience: one path lit by decency, the other shrouded in predation. They did not hesitate. Step by calculated step, they followed, they watched, and they waited – until the moment arrived

> *when temptation eclipsed restraint. The accused, Mr [. . .], did not drift into wrongdoing like a leaf upon a stream; he strode into it with eyes unclouded and moral compass cast aside. The Victim, barely conscious and wholly vulnerable, could neither resist nor consent. Yet he pressed on.*
>
> *When modesty is violated in such a manner, when vulnerability is seized upon with such callous disregard, the law must not whisper. It must speak with a clear, resonant voice, for conduct of this kind tears at the very weave of a civilised society.*

While noting that such introductions can be 'oases in the deserts of legal writing', Professor Berry cautioned about the impact that such an introduction may have on the losing party, and the inevitable discontinuity between such an introduction and the rest of the judgment.[14]

The challenge is to find an appropriate balance between the 'bureaucratic' and 'writerly' introductions. I provide five suggestions to guide this process.

First, write the introduction *last*, after there is a complete draft of the judgment in play, because it is often only at this time that the judicial mind has clarity on what the case is really about, what matters and what does not, and how to frame the dispute as succinctly and effectively as possible.

Second, establish the tone of the judgment early. The tone should be judicious, reflecting respect and humility (as discussed in Chapter 5).

Third, if the case lends itself to a narrative frame, it is fine to tell a story – but guard carefully against sensational language or overstatement (concepts that are discussed at greater detail elsewhere in this book[15]), as well as excessive length. What is needed in the introduction is a concise narrative, not a detailed (or dramatic) saga.

Fourth, do not load the introduction with full quotations (such as statutory text, charges, or evidential matters such as contractual clauses)[16] or with second-order details (such as dates, times, and locations that are not critical for a broad overview).

Fifth, if the judgment turns on a single issue or on a small cluster of issues that sit within an overarching issue, it may be helpful to signal that issue (or those issues) in the introduction. But where the judgment traverses numerous distinct issues, the introduction is rarely the place to catalogue them – attempting to do so risks overwhelming the reader and defeating the purpose of a concise opening.

ORIENTING THE READER: STARTING AT THE END

My preferred fictional reads draw from the detective novel genre. Within this genre, Sherlock Holmes is my perennial favourite, as one may have surmised from my reference to the great detective in Chapter 2. I find Sir Arthur Conan Doyle's narrative style enthralling – drawing the reader steadily through a labyrinth of clues and misdirection, until Holmes, with his trademark flick of certainty, reveals the villain at the end. This approach is not unique to Doyle, of course. I also enjoy the exploits of Agatha Christie's great Belgian detective Hercule Poirot. A common trope in Poirot's adventures is that the reader would be teased with cryptic remarks and dramatic pauses, only for Poirot to unveil the truth in a climactic drawing-room scene, usually with all suspects present and tension thick in the air.[17]

In writing judgments, judges are sometimes guided by the storyteller's instinct: build suspense, save the reveal, and make the reader wait for the final flourish. It can feel satisfying to lay out each strand – the facts, the law, the submissions – and then deliver the punch (i.e., the holding), much like Holmes or Poirot unveiling the culprit. But unlike detective fiction, readers of judgments – especially those to whom the judgments relate – do not appreciate suspense. They need guidance to navigate the judgment, and knowing the endpoint upfront usually helps them to do so.

Stating the conclusion upfront does not rob the judgment of its persuasive force to a reader. Rather, it lends it, for when readers know where a judgment is headed, this helps them to understand how each subsequent step gets the judge there. It eases the cognitive load on the reader. It also signals that the journey is one of purpose, rather than a meandering adventure in search of a conclusion. Having the conclusion upfront also guards against what has been called the 'watch me think' style of judgment writing – a style in which the reader is made to follow the judge's internal deliberations without the benefit of early signposts or a clear structure.[18] As Lady Mary Arden of the UK Supreme Court has observed:[19]

> *The danger in judgment writing is that judges may write in a 'watch me think' style. By that I mean that the reader is bound to follow the writer's process of thought without the conclusions being made clear at an early enough stage and without the ideas being structured for clarity, emphasis, and coherence.*

Beyond helping the reader, stating the conclusion upfront also does something salutary for the judgment writer. It forces the writer to consider whether the path that follows actually arrives at the proclaimed destination.[20] When the holding is stated at the outset, every subsequent paragraph must earn its place in getting the reader there. The writer is compelled to ask, in the course of writing or reviewing what has been written: 'Does this point advance the reasoning?', 'Is this detour necessary?', 'Have I made the connection clear?' In this way, starting at the end helps transform the judgment from a record of thought into a demonstration of thought.

I pause to note that the suggestion to start at the end may not apply with similar force to oral judgments. In spoken delivery, announcing the outcome at the outset may cause the audience – particularly the losing party – to disengage or focus solely on the result, making it more difficult for them to absorb the reasons that follow. In such cases, it may be more effective to build toward the conclusion, guiding the listener through the reasoning step by step before delivering the holding.

MARKING THE PATH: USING CLEAR SIGNPOSTS

The structure of a judgment is most evident from the headings deployed by the writer throughout the judgment. In several judgment writing classes I have taught over the years, I have approached the topic of headings with a personal anecdote.

I enjoy a regular diet of recreational running. These runs do not cease when I travel. Indeed, setting aside time and space for runs on my travels allows me to explore new surroundings briskly and up close, while engaging multi-sensorily with a fresh environment. On one such trip, I set out to run in a tranquil parkland surrounding a beautiful river in Western Australia. The crisp air and beautiful scenery were invigorating as I set out at a good pace, eager to explore while working up a sweat. But as I ran deeper into the park, I began to realise an unanticipated challenge – that there were hardly any directional signs in the park. To compound difficulties, the path frequently branched in two or three directions, offering no indication of where each led. I was initially not overly concerned by this, for I thought that I would eventually be able to retrace my steps and find my way out of the park. I did, however, start making mental notes of visual signposts at each junction – such as a uniquely shaped bush, a small clearing, or a puddle of water on the ground. But as I continued running deeper into the park, I realised that I was losing my grip on these impromptu signposts. The sun began to set, the temperature began to drop, and even my warmed-up body was beginning to feel the wind chill. I became increasingly anxious about my location. The growing darkness added to my disorientation. What had started as an enjoyable evening run had turned into a stressful situation, all because of a lack of clear markers along the way.

Once my watch signalled that I had covered half of my target distance, I turned around to retrace my steps for the second half of my run. Unfortunately, I quickly realised after the first three to four hundred meters of the about-turn that I simply could not remember the way back. Even if I could recall the impromptu signposts in the correct order, things looked very different in the reverse direction, let alone in the fading light. I eventually did successfully exit the park, but found myself some two kilometres away from where I had started, and along a road where I thankfully could be guided by the lights from passing vehicles.

Now, imagine if the park had been well signposted. Signs indicating 'River View Loop ←', 'Exit to Car Park →', or 'East Bridge ↑' would have transformed my experience. I could have made informed decisions about my route, avoided the challenge of holding information about impromptu signposts in my head, enjoyed the run without anxiety, and easily found my way to the end of the run.

Like a parkland with few unique landmarks, a judgment (especially a complex one) can be large, unfamiliar, and filled with turns. Without clear headings to guide and orient, readers are left to wander and wonder, unsure where they are or where they are going. As readers read further, they begin to forget what they read earlier; they may also grow tired and anxious to get through the judgment. Without headings, what should be a carefully guided path becomes a test of stamina and trust. The result, as with my run, is not discovery but discomfort and disorientation.

How Headings Help

Good headings are waypoints for both reader and writer.

For the reader, headings break the judgment into digestible segments and clarify the architecture of the reasoning.[21] They serve as reminders of where a reader is in the overall structure and journey of the judgment, thus helping to maintain context and reducing the likelihood of getting lost.

Admittedly, headings may fragment the reading experience and also encourage a reader to jump to discrete sections in the judgment and possibly read them out of context. As Professor James Raymond cautioned, headings 'will aid those readers who raid your text like marauding pirates, looking for what interests them and ignoring the rest'.[22] This risk cannot be entirely avoided, especially in an age of decreasing attention spans.[23] But the risk of out-of-context reading can be mitigated through the use of clear transitions at the start of each section, possibly including cross-references to earlier or later parts of the judgment so that the reader is reminded to read a specific section in context.

For the writer, headings help to focus the writing process. With headings laid out in a draft judgment, a writer is less likely to let points meander across overlapping areas. Such headings also force the writer to make certain structural decisions, such as: 'What exactly is this section about?', 'Am I moving forward or circling back?', and 'Do I need to revise the structure of the judgment if there are too many overlaps?' If there is a large swathe of text for which one struggles to phrase a heading, it may be a warning sign that one is unclear about the true focus or purpose of the section.

Types of Headings

How, then, should headings be phrased? Different authors utilise different terminology for headings, but I find it useful to think in terms of three broad heading types.[24]

First, *Functional* headings. These mark broad categories, such as 'Background Facts', 'Procedural History', and 'Applicable Legal Framework'. Functional headings are useful for setting up the broad terrain in the judgment and thus work especially well as first-level headings. However, they provide very little detail about what is discussed within the section.

Second, *Descriptive-Objective* headings. These pose a legal or factual question. Examples include 'Whether Agreement was put into writing' and 'Whether Claimant knew that the funds were misappropriated'. They invite focus on the specific issues at hand (thus 'descriptive') without stating any conclusions (thus 'objective').

Third, *Descriptive-Argumentative* headings. These go a step further than Descriptive-Objective headings by offering the judge's conclusion to the identified issue. Adapting from the earlier examples of Descriptive-Objective headings, their Descriptive-Argumentative counterparts would be 'Agreement was never put into writing' and 'Claimant knew that the funds were misappropriated'. Such headings are similar to what is commonly taught in legal writing classes for legal submissions, as they have persuasive force.[25] They help by anchoring each section with a clear outcome in mind. This allows the reader to absorb the direction of the judge's decision before diving into the supporting material.[26] It also signals a sense of progression within the judgment, with each Descriptive-Argumentative heading marking not just a topic, but a resolved point. If such headings are properly used, the architecture of the judgment and the direction of the judge's decision may well be gleaned from perusal of a table of contents that sets out all the headings in the judgment.

Some have expressed reservations – among them participants in judgment writing classes I have taught – about whether Descriptive-Argumentative headings are suitable for judgments, given their association with written advocacy. In contrast, Functional or Descriptive-Objective headings convey a greater sense of detached neutrality, aligning more closely with the judicial role. While there is force in this concern, it does not follow that Descriptive-Argumentative headings should be avoided altogether. As discussed in Chapters 1 and 2 earlier, there is room – indeed utility – for a judgment to persuade.[27] Whether that persuasion is best achieved through the quiet authority of objective framing or through headings that reflect the judge's conclusion depends on the nature of the issue, the structure of the judgment, and the intended rhetorical effect. The choice is not binary but contextual. What matters is that the heading serves the reader's understanding and reflects the judgment's tone, stage, and purpose.

Ultimately, there is no formulaic way to select the most appropriate type of headings for each use case. There is a degree of subjectivity in the preferred style of headings to adopt, and what really matters is intentionality –meaning that each heading is selected to serve the purpose of guiding the reader through the judgment. In practice, a thoughtful mix of different types of headings probably works best for most judgments. As an example, see *Eugene Phoa v Oey Liang Ho*,[28] where the court adopted a mix of Functional, Descriptive-Objective, and Descriptive-Argumentative headings.

- **[INTRODUCTION]** *(The actual judgment does not apply an 'Introduction' heading, but the first two paragraphs of the judgment are of an introductory nature)*
- **THE PARTIES**
  - **The Phoas**
  - **The Kasendas**
  - **Supratechnic**
- **THE PROCEDURAL HISTORY**
- **THE PARTIES' GENERAL POSITIONS**
  - **Eugene's Claimed Reliefs**

- LOT A SHARES
- LOT B SHARES
- LOT C SHARES
- SUBSEQUENT PERIOD AFTER EVELYN'S DEATH
- SUMMARY OF PLEADED CASES
- SUMMARY OF THE RELEVANT DOCUMENTS

- THE RELEVANT ISSUES
- WHETHER EUGENE HAS STANDING TO PURSUE THE CLAIMS IN THIS SUIT
- WHETHER EUGENE'S CLAIMS ARE TIME-BARRED
  - THE PARTIES' POSITIONS
  - THE APPLICABLE PROVISIONS
  - MY DECISION: EUGENE'S CLAIMS ARE TIME-BARRED
    - *Sections 22(1) and 22(2) of the LA*
    - *Section 24A(3) of the LA*
    - *Section 29(1) of the LA*
    - *The Canadian proceedings did not affect the time-bar*
    - The only claim that is potentially not time-barred
- WHETHER EUGENE'S CLAIMS ARE BARRED BY LACHES
  - THE PARTIES' POSITIONS
  - MY DECISION: EUGENE'S CLAIMS ARE BARRED BY LACHES
    - *The applicable law*
    - *Eugene had unjustifiably delayed commencing this Suit*
    - *There is clear prejudice to the defendants*
- NOTWITHSTANDING THE PROCEDURAL ISSUES, WHETHER EUGENE'S CLAIM IN RELATION TO THE LOT C SHARES SUCCEEDS
  - THE PARTIES' GENERAL POSITIONS
  - MY DECISION: EUGENE'S CLAIM TO THE LOT C SHARES FAILS BECAUSE WIRIO NEVER BREACHED ANY DUTY AS A BARE TRUSTEE
    - *Evelyn's Estate is not estopped from contending that Wirio was a trustee for Evelyn*
    - *Wirio never breached any duty as a bare trustee over the Lot C shares*
    - *No findings in relation to alleged tax evasion*
- NOTWITHSTANDING THE PROCEDURAL ISSUES, WHETHER EUGENE'S CLAIM IN CONVERSION SUCCEEDS
- CONCLUSION

Depth and Breadth of Headings

The example from *Eugene Phoa v Oey Liang Ho* also offers food for thought on the number of heading levels. Earlier, I set out three levels of judgment from the case. The actual judgment had a fourth level of headings. This raises a point for consideration: how many levels of headings is too much?

My omission of the fourth level of headings is not intended as a comment that four levels are too much. Indeed, the Singapore judgment template's stylesheet accommodates up to eight levels (albeit as a matter of technical formatting capacity, not recommendation),[29] while other recognised law journal or formal academic writing style guides offer four or more levels of headings.[30] Leading law journals do not appear to prescribe a maximum number of heading levels, although some law journals suggest that there should not be more than four levels of headings.[31]

The point I wish to make is that deeply nested headings can create cognitive fatigue. They may obscure rather than illuminate, especially if the reader struggles to recall where they are within the judgment's architecture. A heading should orient the reader, not require them to decode a hierarchy. If a section requires multiple sub-sub-headings to stay organised, it may be worth asking whether the material can be simplified, restructured, or broken into more coherent thematic units.

This concern with heading hierarchy applies not only to how deep the structure goes but also to how balanced it is.

Structural imbalance can arise when headings are used unnecessarily or unevenly – particularly in sections where the analysis is brief or straightforward. For instance, sub-headings may not be needed where there is only a single paragraph of text under each heading, or where the material is better presented as a list of items each followed by brief content (rather than short paragraphs or sentences organised under multiple headings).

An even more obvious sign of structural imbalance in headings is the use of a solitary sub-heading. For if there is only one sub-point, this may not warrant a separate sub-heading at all. Headings are most useful when they help the reader distinguish between multiple components within a broader category. A single sub-heading, by contrast, may suggest that the writer is over-segmenting the material, has not yet clarified the internal logic of the section, or has omitted a sub-section (either erroneously or by virtue of a belated decision to remove a sub-section without revisiting the structure as a whole). In such cases, it is often better to integrate the content into the main body of the section or to reconsider whether the section itself should be reframed or subdivided differently. As always, the test is whether the breadth and depth of headings serve the reader's understanding.

CLEARING THE CLUTTER: AVOIDING THE KITCHEN SINK APPROACH

There is a lawyerly instinct, particularly when writing judgments in complex or contentious cases, to include absolutely everything – every argument raised, every authority cited, every side alley explored during the hearing, or even every detour engaged in the judge's mind. The temptation can come from a good place, such as the desire to be thorough or to honour the parties' efforts. But it may also stem from a desire to avoid the discipline of tightening the judgment or a misplaced belief that comprehensiveness helps the judgment survive appellate scrutiny (i.e., to 'appeal proof' the judgment).

Unfortunately, throwing in every piece of analysis does not make a judgment tight or more 'appeal proof'. It may in fact make it looser, more opaque, and more questionable on appeal. It burdens the reader, including the appellate court, with trying to make sense of what mattered and what did not (and I know from conversations with numerous apex court judges that such a burden is generally not appreciated). It risks turning the judgment into a 'watch me think' exercise, where the reader is forced to follow the judge's internal deliberations.[32]

Restraining oneself from throwing in everything but the kitchen sink (or even the kitchen sink itself) requires courage. It requires the courage to omit what does not serve the reasoning. It requires the courage to trust that the judgment will stand not because it mentions every possible point, but because it persuades on the ones that matter. This is not about brevity for its own sake. It is about restraint in the service of readability.

The practices suggested earlier in this chapter – adopting an Issue-Driven approach in appropriate cases, using headings, stating conclusions upfront – can help the writer to produce a more structurally sound and focused judgment, which can also serve as a form of restraint against throwing in the kitchen sink. Here, I offer three further practical suggestions on resisting the temptation to throw everything into a written judgment.

First, avoid over-citation. Cite only the authorities that materially support the reasoning. A long string of cases may signal insecurity rather than strength. It can also obscure the key precedent or principle by burying it in a crowd. Selectivity is not a weakness. It is a mark of confidence and clarity. Indeed, in the Singapore Supreme Court, counsel who wish to cite more than two judgments as authority for a given proposition must provide in their submissions a compelling reason to do so.[33] Judges, too, would do well to adopt this as a best practice by resisting the urge to cite exhaustively, and instead curate authorities with the reader's clarity in mind.

Second, apply the test of relevance or materiality – tests which judges should be intimately familiar with, from ruling on document production, admissibility, and other evidentiary matters. When drafting or reviewing the judgment, ask: 'Does this advance the explanation?' or 'Is this necessary for resolving the issue?' If the answer is 'no', omit it. This test helps the writer distinguish between what is interesting and what is essential. It also encourages a reader-centred discipline: every paragraph must earn its place.

Third, be cautious when presenting multiple pathways and alternatives. It is not uncommon for judges to present several alternative routes that lead to the same outcome. Properly used, this helps reinforce the result and demonstrate the robustness of reasoning. But if the judgment explores the alternative pathways in too much detail or disproportionately to the main line of reasoning, it may risk confusing the reader as to what the primary decision or reasoning is. On a related note, if the pathways diverge or lead to different outcomes, there may be a temptation to address them all to show that the judge has considered every possibility. This instinct, while intellectually generous, may not be particularly useful to the reader and, if not managed carefully, may give the appearance of hedging rather than deciding.

CONCLUDING REFLECTIONS

Tight writing – writing that is properly structured, signposted, and sorted – takes time. It certainly takes far more time than writing loosely. It requires the writer to make decisions about what to include, what to omit, and how to group ideas in ways that will serve the reader. I have winced when I re-read some of my past judgments – not because I have changed my mind about the outcome, but because of the way I allowed the judgment to meander for too long. In those instances, I unfortunately wrote for myself, not for the reader.

Tight writing is the judicial equivalent of tidying a room. The reader enters the judgment as one might enter a space: hoping to understand what happened here, and how. If the facts, laws, submissions, and findings are strewn across the floor, the reader's patience is tested and understanding compromised. But when the judgment is structured with intention, each item has its place. Through a tight judgment, the judge tells the reader: 'I have done the hard work of tidying, so you don't have to'. The act of tightening the judgment contributes towards chaos becoming clarity.

NOTES

1 Marie Kondo, *Spark Joy: An Illustrated Guide to the Japanese Art of Tidying* (Vermillion 2017).

2 Deborah Linton, 'How Marie Kondo Changed Her Mind About Mess: "I Realised Perfect Order Was Not My Goal – It Was Spending Time With My Kids"' *The Guardian* (30 March 2024) <https://perma.cc/U6Y8-TN33>.

3 Edward Berry, *Writing Reasons: A Handbook for Judges* (6th edn, LexisNexis Canada 2025) 25.

4 Berry (n 3) 26.

5 *Public Prosecutor v Henry Koh Yik Wee* [2025] SGMC 64.

6 Berry (n 3) 27. Professor Berry attributes the terminology of 'proximity' to Justice John Laskin of the Court of Appeal for Ontario.

7 Professor Edward Berry discussed a similar model, albeit in the context of the Issues-Driven approach. See Berry (n 3) 29–30.

8 *Public Prosecutor v Ridhaudin Ridhwan bin Bakri* [2019] SGHC 105.

9 *Eugene Phoa (personal representative of the estate of Evelyn Phoa @ Lauw, Evelyn Siew Chiang, deceased, and personal representative of the estate of William Phoa, deceased) v Oey Liang Ho @ Henry Kasenda (sole executor of the estate of Wirio Kasenda @ Oey Giok Tjeng, deceased)* [2024] SGHC 22. The full extent of the judgment is found in the unreported version of the judgment (with the neutral citation as stated in this footnote); the reported version of the judgment ([2024] 4 SLR 1493) is limited only to selected issues.

10 As Professor Edward Berry observes, sometimes the Issue-Driven approach 'must be adapted', or sometimes it 'simply won't work': Berry (n 3) 31.

11 Berry (n 3) 14.

12 Berry (n 3) 14–15.

13 This is the same judgment used to generate the 'Denning-esque' introduction in Chapter 8 (on 'The Appeal of Assistants').

14 Berry (n 3) 15.

15 On sensationalism, see Chapter 5 (on 'Rhetorical Choice'); on overstatement, see Chapter 4 (on 'Guarding Against Hedging or Overstatement').

16 In James Raymond, 'The Architecture of Argument' (2004) 7 The Judicial Review: Journal of the Judicial Commission of New South Wales 39, 51, the author suggests that avoiding citing specific sections of the relevant legislation is a useful way to avoid cluttering the opening paragraph.

17 I note with some amusement that I wrote this segment of the book on board a flight, shortly before enjoying the film *A Haunting in Venice* that was incidentally available on in-flight entertainment. The finale of the movie satisfyingly validated the main text accompanying this footnote.

18 Mary Arden, *Shaping Tomorrow's Law: Common Law and Modern Society – Keeping Pace With Change*, vol 2 (Oxford University Press 2015) 239.

19 Arden (n 18) 239.

20 See Chapter 1 (on 'Encouraging Accuracy') and Chapter 2 (on 'The Need for Explanation').

21 This point is emphasised in many texts, articles, and speeches about good judgment writing. See e.g. Lord Burrows, 'Judgment Writing: A Personal Perspective' (Speech at the Annual Conference of Judges of the Superior Courts in Ireland, 20 May 2021) <https://perma.cc/7LY4-YRAS> 2, 3.

22 Raymond (n 16) 48.

23 See Chapter 7.

24 For instance, in Raymond (n 16) 47–49, the author suggests that there are two kinds of headings: 'generic' and 'case specific'. For the 'case specific' type of headings, the author further suggests three sub-types: phrasing as an 'argument', as a 'question', or as a 'topic'.

25 See e.g. Bryan A Garner, *Legal Writing in Plain English: A Text With Exercises* (3rd edn, The University of Chicago Press 2023) 28 on the use of 'point headings' (that is, a full-sentence proposition that advances a premise, which together form a cohesive outline of the legal case).

26 A point discussed in the previous section, 'Orienting the Reader: Starting at the End'.

27 See the discussion in Chapter 1 (on 'Promoting Transparency and Accountability') and Chapter 2.

28 *Eugene Phoa* (n 9).

29 When I first developed the Singapore judiciary's judgment template, it had only five levels of headings. This was subsequently increased to eight as judgments became lengthier and more complex.

30 See, for instance, the American Psychological Association style (often referred to as 'APA style' or 'APA format'), which applies to academic documents particularly within the social sciences. The APA style affords up to five levels of heading: see American Psychological Association, 'APA Style: Headings' <https://perma.cc/P4GR-9J3P>.

31 See the Singapore Journal of Legal Studies style guidelines: Singapore Journal of Legal Studies, 'Style Guidelines' <https://perma.cc/6TYC-YPS6>, which states 'The levels of headings should not exceed four'.

32 See 'Orienting the Reader: Starting at the End' earlier.

33 Supreme Court Practice Directions 2021 (Singapore) para 106(2).

Getting to the Point – Writing Precisely and Concisely

Four

In my youth, I enjoyed weekends shaped by dice rolls and the simple joy of a well-designed boardgame. As life quickened its pace, however, I have found it harder to carve out the hours that boardgames require. The prospect of learning a *new* boardgame is even more daunting – with the need to figure out unfamiliar game mechanics, rules, and exceptions, this often feels like more trouble than it is worth.

So when a family member suggested trying a boardgame we had never played before, I was sceptical. *Nanty Narking*, a Victorian-era strategy boardgame set in the streets of London, was not one of the well-known games. The box was beautifully illustrated, and the gameplay looked elaborate: hidden roles, character cards, and area control mechanics, just to name a few. I wondered how long it would take to learn the rules and whether it would be worth the effort. I agreed only because of the setting. I have always had a soft spot for the Victorian-era literary classics – Dickens, Doyle, and the fog-drenched streets of London. *Nanty Narking* promised a world drawn from that literary imagination. Paired with a few atmospheric soundtracks in the background[1] – horse-drawn carriages, distant bells, and the occasional street cry – I braced myself to figure out the rules of the game.

To my surprise, the rulebook was clear, concise, and easy to follow. Written for a general audience aged 14 and above, it struck an optimal balance: accessible to the uninitiated, yet not oversimplified. It anticipated confusion before it arose, using point-form instructions, visuals, and examples to illustrate how the rules worked in practice. Little wonder, then, that in *Writing to Win*, Steven Stark observed that some of the clearest technical writing appears in boardgame instructions.[2] The goal in judgment writing is somewhat similar: to guide the lay reader in an unfamiliar and complex territory with precision and concision.

Justice Andrew Phang has often emphasised the need to write 'simply without being simplistic'.[3] While he is probably not the first to have used this phrase, it is through his commitment to this ethic that it has come to resonate most deeply with me. It captures a deceptively difficult

DOI: 10.4324/9781042017027-5

standard. Writing simply requires effort (in both possible readings of that phrase). It is not the absence of complexity, but the discipline of expressing complexity in a way that remains accessible and accurate. It is not a lowering of standards, but a raising of them, anchored in a commitment to the twin aims of precision and concision.

This chapter explores how precision and concision can be achieved in judicial writing. It begins with techniques for sentence construction that help writers express their reasoning with focus and flow. It then examines the dangers of hedging and overstatement, offering strategies for making one's point without sounding evasive or excessive. From there, it addresses forms of legal excess – whether in the guise of metadiscourse or legalese – that obscure meaning in written judgments. Finally, it considers how judges can explain technical or unfamiliar subject matter in a way that remains accessible to lay readers, drawing on techniques that help illuminate rather than intimidate.

MAKING SENTENCES WORK

The sentence is the basic building block of each written judgment. However complex the legal issues, however layered the reasoning, the judgment is ultimately constructed one sentence at a time. Precision and concision at the sentence level is therefore not a matter of style alone; it affects the very focus and flow of the judgment.

The art of sentence construction is a field of study in itself. These technical aspects are certainly important for improving our writing and are discussed in detail by many who specialise in the craft of writing.[4] My aim here, however, is more modest – to reflect on four simple but powerful techniques of sentence organisation that help reduce the cognitive load placed upon readers: keeping subject and verb together, avoiding mid-sentence detours, leading with the main clause, and managing sentence length.

Keeping Subject and Verb Together

One of the rudiments involves keeping subject and verb close together. When this is done, the reader is not left waiting for the point. This is a small choice in sentence structure, but it can make a significant difference to how well a sentence flows.

Indeed, simple adjustments to the placement of subjects and verbs can help make our writing more concise – not necessarily by reducing the word count, but by reducing the distance between expression and comprehension. We can achieve economy of expression even without achieving economy in word count.

Take this sentence, for instance:

> *The court, after reviewing all the evidence and considering the child's best interests, awards custody to the mother.*

Now, compare it with:

> *After reviewing all the evidence and considering the child's best interests, the court awards custody to the mother.*

Both sentences comprise exactly 18 words. All 18 words are identical. The only difference is a minor reordering of the words. The subject ('the court') and the verb ('awards') are now no longer separated by a long intervention. The example demonstrates that bringing subject and verb into closer proximity produces a sentence that reads with greater precision and concision.

Avoiding Mid-Sentence Detours

A sentence can lose focus if it is cluttered with embedded clauses, parentheticals, or rhetorical asides. These mid-sentence detours fracture rhythm, obscure logic, and distract from the main point.

By keeping subject and verb together as suggested in the first technique, writers are prompted to scrutinise more closely whatever they place in the intervening space. Very often, it is in that space (i.e., between subject and verb) that one may be tempted to insert clauses, conditions, qualifications, and context. The more space one allows between subject and verb, the more tempted one is to over-explain, to hedge, to insert parenthetical comments or to defer the point. And the more one does that, the more meandering or obscure the sentence becomes.

Drawing on the same example used previously, we can see how the interruption grows when we fail to keep subject-verb proximity:

> *The court, after reviewing all the evidence submitted by both parties, including affidavits, expert reports, and oral testimony, and having considered the relevant statutory provisions and case law, as well as the child's educational and emotional needs, awards custody to the mother.*

The sentence is still grammatically and substantively correct. But the main point – what the court decided – is now further buried in a 42-word sentence. The reader is forced to work to reconstruct the key point of the sentence. And the writer, in trying to be thorough, may have lost sight of the crux of the sentence.

Of course, there are times when qualifiers or context are necessary. But even then, a writer should ask whether those qualifiers or contextual references belong *within* the sentence or *after* it. Not every detail needs to interrupt the core message.

Consider this sentence:

> *The claimant, who had previously been warned about the risks (and who, incidentally, had ignored similar advice in the past), failed to mitigate his losses.*

Now, compare it with:

> *The claimant failed to mitigate his losses. He had previously been warned about the risks and had ignored similar advice.*

The revised version separates the main point from its supporting context. It allows each idea to breathe, and avoids burying the core message – *the claimant failed to mitigate* – under layers of commentary.

Mid-sentence detours often arise from a desire to be thorough. But thoroughness need not mean convolution. As Bo Seo has observed from the world of competitive debating, at the sentence level, qualifications and counterpoints should wait until the main point is established; otherwise, '[i]n a bid to be faultless we fail the more basic task of getting the message out'.[5] The same discipline applies in judgment writing. When the core of the sentence is clear, elaboration can follow without disruption. The discipline lies in knowing when to pause, when to separate, and when to let the sentence arrive before it expands.

Leading With the Main Clause

Leading with the main clause helps anchor the sentence and reduce cognitive load. Otherwise, when a sentence begins with subordinate clauses, background context, elaboration, or qualifiers, the reader must hold all that in working memory before reaching the main point. This can be cognitively taxing, especially when the sentence is long or the context unfamiliar.

Consider this example:

> *Although the defendant had previously complied with similar orders, and despite the mitigating circumstances raised, the court found that a custodial sentence was warranted.*

Now, compare it with:

> *The court found that a custodial sentence was warranted, despite the mitigating circumstances raised and the defendant's prior compliance.*

The second version foregrounds the court's decision, before elaborating on it. It helps the reader grasp the judgment's direction before processing its nuance. This structure is especially useful when the main clause is short and the qualifiers or elaborations are long.

Managing Sentence Length

A single long sentence can sometimes feel like a marathon. The reader must hold multiple ideas, clauses, and qualifications in working memory before reaching the finish line. Again, this increases cognitive load and risks obscuring the main point.

By contrast, using a few short sentences often achieves greater clarity. This allows each idea to stand on its own, reduces the chance of misinterpretation, and gives the reader natural pauses to absorb the reasoning. Shorter sentences also create rhythm and momentum, which can be especially valuable in judgments where the reader is navigating complex legal terrain.

Keep each sentence focused on a single idea, aiming for an average length of 20–35 words.[6] Balance shorter and longer sentences to create rhythm and prevent the text from sounding abrupt or overly clipped.

The discipline lies not in avoiding long sentences altogether, but in recognising when a thought is better expressed in a few crisp statements rather than one sprawling construction. Consider this example:

> The defendant, having failed to comply with the interim orders despite repeated opportunities to do so, and having disregarded the warnings issued by the court, was found to have acted in contempt and was accordingly sentenced to a term of imprisonment.

Now, compare it with:

> The court found the defendant in contempt and sentenced him to imprisonment. He failed to comply with the interim orders despite repeated opportunities and disregarded the court's warnings.

Sentence length is ultimately about respecting the reader's cognitive effort. A judgment that strings together multiple clauses in a single breath may demonstrate thoroughness, but it risks exhausting the reader before the point is clear. The craft lies in balance – knowing when a thought deserves its own sentence, when rhythm calls for variation, and when a longer construction is justified.

SAYING WHAT WE MEAN

It is oft said that we should say what we mean and mean what we say. However, as legal writers exposed to (or perhaps schooled in) the art of caveating on the one hand and grandstanding on the other, we sometimes fail to do so. We struggle with two opposing tendencies: hedging and overstatement.

Hedging

As legal writers, we are cautious by instinct. We want to be fair. We want to acknowledge complexity and nuance. But in trying to do so, we sometimes end up saying *less* than we mean, or saying it *less clearly* than we should. The most obvious form of hedging behaviour is in the indiscriminate use of qualifiers: 'arguably', 'somewhat', and 'may not have been'. These phrases can obscure the points we are trying to make.

Consider this (exaggerated) example:

> *The defendant's conduct arguably breached the duty of care. While there may have been some mitigating circumstances, he did not appear to meet the standard expected of a reasonable person. It could be said that the failure to act more promptly probably contributed to the harm suffered.*

Now, compare it with:

> *The defendant breached the duty of care. Although there were mitigating circumstances, he failed to meet the standard expected of a reasonable person. The failure to act promptly contributed to the harm suffered.*

In the first version, the writer hedges at nearly every turn. The conduct 'arguably' breached the duty of care; he 'did not appear to meet' the standard; the failure to act 'probably contributed' to the harm. Each phrase introduces uncertainty because of its less committal language. The cumulative effect is a paragraph that feels tentative or equivocal. While this may be justified when there is a lack of clarity on the issue in question, a writer must guard against the habitual use of such qualifiers simply because one is reluctant to commit to a clear position. When overused, hedging language can obscure the strength of the reasoning and leave the reader unsure of what the writer actually thinks. It also risks frustrating the reader, who must work harder to discern the writer's meaning.

The revised version, by contrast, is more confident and direct. It acknowledges mitigating circumstances but does not let them dilute the conclusion. Instead, it states unequivocally that the standard was not met, and that the failure to act contributed to the harm.

Overstatement

The opposite danger to hedging is overstatement – that is, the overuse of intensifiers and absolutes. Words such as 'clearly', 'manifestly', or 'undoubtedly' may sound decisive, but they can also suggest a level of certainty that neither the facts nor the law support. Litigants whose arguments are dismissed as 'manifestly without merit' may feel not only that they have lost, but that their position has not been understood.[7]

Consider the following sentence:

> *The claimant's arguments are entirely baseless and reflect a fundamental misunderstanding of the law.*

Now, compare it with:

> *The claimant's arguments find no support in the cited authorities and reflect a misunderstanding of the law.*

The original version not only dismisses the arguments, but it also implies incompetence or intellectual failure. Unless this is what is intended and can be justified in the circumstances, it risks sounding punitive rather than principled, and may leave the losing party feeling dismissed rather than heard. I discuss a related point from the angle of avoiding sarcasm or ridicule, in Chapter 5. The revised version is stronger, offering firmness without the intensifiers that can make a judgment sound more emphatic than warranted.

More subtly, overstatement can give the impression that the decision was easy or obvious, when in truth, it may not have been so. Judicial reasoning can (and often does) involve genuine struggle: weighing competing authorities, navigating factual uncertainty, and confronting the limits of legal doctrine. When we overstate the ease of reaching the outcome, we risk erasing the difficulty of the path that led there and suggesting (wrongly) that one side was plainly right and the other plainly without merit.

Guarding Against Hedging or Overstatement

How do we guard against hedging or overstatement? While much of this resists formula and is honed by experience, there are three practical techniques that can be helpful.

First, read the sentence aloud. Tone often reveals itself more clearly to the ear than to the eye. A written sentence that sounds evasive or overbearing when spoken may need revision. Reading aloud can help surface unintended implications, whether these may communicate excessive caution or undue certainty.

Second, test the sentence without the qualifier or intensifier. Remove the word or phrase in question (e.g., 'arguably', 'clearly', 'somewhat', 'manifestly') and ask – 'does the sentence still accurately reflect how confident I feel about the point?' If so, the modifier may be unnecessary, or even misleading.

Third, ask if the sentence clarifies the strength of the reasoning or compensates for its weakness. If the reasoning is substantively strong, it seldom needs to be declared 'clear' or 'obvious' (unless those are themselves the legal tests or touchstones). If the reasons are less robust, pause to consider: 'am I asserting strength to reassure myself, or to persuade the reader, because the reasoning may not fully sustain what I claim?'

These techniques can help resist the pull of habit – whether toward hedging or overstatement. They encourage us to reflect on whether our word choices truly convey what we really think and mean.

LOSING THE LEGAL EXCESS

Even when our sentence structures are sound and our word choices convey what we mean, our writing can still be overrun by the use of unfamiliar words and phrases. An empirical study of two decades[8] of judgments from the Singapore Supreme Court (which comprises the High Court and the Court of Appeal) found that these judgments tended to 'contain more unfamiliar or difficult words, and have longer sentences on average when compared to newspaper articles on similar topics'.[9] To be sure, many of these judgments do engage with complex and technical legal issues and doctrinal nuance, and probably cannot be expected to read as simply as newspaper articles. That said, the study serves as a reminder to be mindful of how unfamiliar words and extended constructions affect readability.

To illustrate how linguistic clutter can obscure meaning, consider the following paragraph (which is slightly exaggerated from examples I have come across – but only slightly):

> *Before proceeding to the dispositive issues herein, it is submitted that the claimant, inter alia, alleges breach of fiduciary duty and misrepresentation, which, prima facie, may be said to impugn the defendant's bona fides. The court, not unmindful of the aforementioned averments, observes that the equities are not entirely aligned in the claimant's favour.*

Now, compare it with:

> *The claimant alleges, among other things, breach of fiduciary duty and misrepresentation. At first glance, these may suggest that the defendant acted in bad faith. However, the equities do not entirely favour the claimant.*

The first version is grammatically correct and formally structured, but its meaning is obscured by layers of Latinisms, legalisms, and abstract phrasing. Words like *inter alia*, *prima facie*, and *bona fides* may be familiar to lawyers, but their cumulative effect – especially when paired with phrases like 'it is submitted that' and 'not unmindful of the aforementioned averments' – is to distance the reader from the substance of the point.

The revised version pares back the language without sacrificing precision. It foregrounds the ideas with plain and accurate terms ('among other things', 'at first glance', and 'acted in bad faith').

There may well be other ways to improve the original paragraph, but the point of this illustration is to home in on three specific forms of linguistic clutter: metadiscourse, legalese, and verbosity. These are especially persistent in legal and judicial writing. They often appear not because they serve the reasoning, but because they echo the habits and conventions of legal style and tradition. Unfortunately, they often undermine both precision and concision.

Metadiscourse

Metadiscourse refers to language that comments on the writing or argument itself.[10] It operates one level above the content – hence 'meta' – and can serve useful purposes: guiding the reader, signalling structure, or framing transitions. But when overused or formulaic, metadiscourse becomes linguistic clutter. These have been likened to 'throat-clearing'[11] linguistic devices – unnecessary ways of easing into a point.

Judges sometimes use phrases such as 'in this court's considered opinion, the respondent's conduct was unreasonable', when it would be clearer and more concise to simply state 'the respondent's conduct was unreasonable'. This revised version is not only shorter but also stronger. It directs attention to the reasoning itself, rather than to the court's manner of presenting it. Furthermore, the phrase 'in this court's considered opinion' adds little for the reader – after all, the reader already expects that judicial opinions are issued only after proper consideration.

Judgments also sometimes include sentences such as 'it is trite to observe that the burden of proof lies with the prosecution'. Would it not be better to simply say 'the burden of proof lies with the prosecution'? This revision states the principle plainly, without the metadiscursive preamble. As with the earlier example, the phrase 'it is trite to observe' adds little to the meaning. It even risks sounding dismissive or self-congratulatory, as if the court was above stating the obvious (while, ironically, doing so).

Another oft-deployed piece of metadiscourse begins with 'it goes without saying'. While this is acceptable in speech, it is rarely necessary on the page. Indeed, does it not go without saying that one need not say something that goes without saying?

These examples show how metadiscourse can quietly accumulate across a judgment. There is no single 'guilty' phrase, but rather a pattern of rhetorical preambles that however familiar or authoritative sounding add little to the substance of the judgment. Minimising such metadiscourse can help achieve greater precision and concision in writing.

Legalese

Legalese refers to the archaic or inflated language (e.g., 'hereby', 'hereinafter', etc.) and Latin terms (e.g., '*a fortiori*', '*mutatis mutandis*', etc.[12]) that continue to appear in contemporary judicial writing. Their continued appearance is driven not only by familiarity within legal circles but also because they sound authoritative and may be perceived to lend a form of inherited legitimacy. After all, they signal tradition, formality, fluency, and expertise in the language of the law.

However, while law prides itself on technical precision, legalese often muddles clarity. We should resist the temptation to occlude our judgments one 'hereinafter' at a time.

There have long been calls for judges and lawyers to write in plain English.[13] Writing in plain language aids comprehension, especially for readers who have not had a legal education. Today, legislation is increasingly written in plain English,[14] and there are various resources or lexicons that guide the use and avoidance of common legal Latinisms.[15]

To be clear, this is not a call to abandon legal language altogether. Some such language carries precise meaning that would be difficult to replicate without distortion or cumbersome explanation. These are better understood as legal 'terms of art'.[16] A common example is '*mens rea*', which refers to the mental state required for legal culpability. Another example is '*sub judice*', which refers to matters currently under judicial consideration and therefore subject to restrictions on public comment. In such cases, a useful approach is to retain the term of art, but pair it with a plain-language explanation that helps the lay reader understand its significance.[17]

The crux is to be critical and judicious about the Latin terms we use, and to avoid them unless they are essential to the judgment. A useful test is to ask: if this term or phrase is removed, does the meaning change? If not, why is it there? If the phrase is doing no substantive work, then it may be worthwhile omitting it. It requires discipline and effort to cull our text for legalese that should be left out. But with practice, the task becomes more manageable.

Verbosity

A third type of linguistic clutter involves phrases that neither comment on the writing itself (as metadiscourse does) nor draw their authority from legal tradition or Latin (as legalese does). Rather, they are needlessly long-winded expressions that can be replaced by simpler, leaner alternatives without any loss of meaning.

These expressions often masquerade as formal or precise, but in truth add little or no value. They have been likened to 'junk food': comforting, familiar, and easy to reach for, but ultimately lacking in substance.[18] Consider the following examples:

> *Until such time → Until*
> *For the reason that → Because*
> *In the event that → If*
> *Despite the fact that → Although*
> *[The list can go on]*

Each of the longer phrases may sound more formal, but none is more precise than its shorter (and more concise) counterpart. The discipline here, as with metadiscourse and legalese, lies in resisting the pull of the familiar, by asking ourselves: 'Can this phrase be shortened without loss of meaning?'

EXPLAINING THE COMPLEX STUFF

The world we live in is increasingly complex. One of the critical challenges that confronts judiciaries all around the world is that of escalating complexity. I have elsewhere discussed this challenge from five different angles.[19] In gist, judges struggle with complexity arising from the expanding scope of scientific and technological knowledge required to resolve disputes, novel issues that challenge the understanding and application of existing legal principles, the cross-border nature of many disputes, the volume and nature of evidence, and the evolving profile of litigants.

When it comes to writing reasons, the judge must undertake the unenviable task of explaining complex matters as comprehensibly as possible. This demands not only that the judge have a good grasp of the subject matter (which may be technical or unfamiliar to the judge) but also the ability to make this intelligible to the lay reader who may not share the judge's background, vocabulary, or understanding of the matter.

The prerequisite to explaining complexity is that the judge first understands the material. A useful test is to see if one can effectively explain the complexities and technicalities in one's own words. If the best one can do is to repeat what counsel or an expert has said, that may be a warning sign that one does not sufficiently understand the matter to explain or even to adjudicate upon it. In such cases, judges should not shy away from seeking clarification from counsel or experts. For example, in *IIa Technologies Pte Ltd v Element Six Technologies Ltd*,[20] the Singapore Court of Appeal convened a 'Technology Tutorial' to deepen its grasp of the technical issues before adjudicating the matter.[21] Seeking clarification is not an admission of weakness; rather, it is an act of care towards justice, the law, and the parties.

A good example of the court explaining a technical term in its own words is found in the Singapore Court of Appeal's decision of *Quoine Pte Ltd v B2C2 Ltd*.[22] This is a landmark appellate decision from the first cryptocurrency trial heard in the Singapore courts,[23] in which the judges had to grapple with the interface between emerging technology and established legal principles.[24] The software in question deployed a 'deterministic' algorithm, which was a characteristic that was significant to the court's analysis. This is how the court explained that characteristic:[25]

> *[T]he Trading Software's algorithm is deterministic . . . which, as defined by both the Judge and [the independent counsel], is one which will always produce precisely the same output given the same input. To put it another way, the Trading Software will do just what it was programmed to do and does not have the capacity to develop its own responses to varying conditions. Hence, faced with any given set of conditions, it will always respond to that in the same way.*

As evident from this passage, the court did not treat the technical term as self-explanatory. Nor did it rely solely on cross-referencing the trial judge's explanation or the definition provided by the independent counsel (previously known as '*amicus curiae*'). Instead, it took pains to explain the concept in its own words, using plain language that is accessible to most lay readers.

Once the judge understands the technical matter well enough to explain it in the judge's own words, the next challenge is how best to craft the explanation so that it can be more easily understood by readers. In the sections that follow, I reflect on four techniques that can help make complex subject matter more comprehensible: using shorthand, lists, tables, and visual tools.

Reducing Repetition With Shorthand

One way of making complex subject matter more accessible is to reduce the burden of repetition by using shorthand for references that repeatedly appear throughout the judgment. Shorthand, when introduced carefully, can help simplify complexity without sacrificing accuracy.

The standard practice is to spell out the term in full the first time it appears, followed by the shorthand in parentheses. For example:

> The Corruption, Drug Trafficking And Other Serious Crimes (Confiscation of Benefits) Act ('CDSA') introduced a new framework for the confiscation of benefits of crime. Under the CDSA, it is an offence to . . .

Judges often use shorthand for repeated references to authorities such as legislation, subsidiary legislation, cases, and secondary authorities. However, shorthand can be usefully deployed beyond this.

One of the areas relates to case elements, such as references to parties, charges, claims, pleadings, and so on. Take, for instance, a situation where a judgment involves multiple parties. Procedural designations such as 'the 1st Defendant in Counterclaim' may be technically correct, but often require the reader to jump through mental hoops to understand which party is being referred to. By contrast, using the party's name ('Mr Yeo') or a capacity that is meaningful in context ('Fourth Uncle') makes the narrative clearer, as the judgment references recognisable figures rather than procedural designations.

It is useful to illustrate this with a pair of examples. The first shows how procedural designations can quickly become cumbersome and difficult to follow:

> The 1st Defendant in Counterclaim filed an application to strike out the counterclaim brought by the Plaintiff in Counterclaim, while the 2nd Defendant in Counterclaim sought document production against the Plaintiff (who is also the 1st Defendant in Counterclaim).

Now compare it with the following (assume that the various parties had earlier been defined by reference to their last names):

> *Mr Yeo filed an application to strike out the counterclaim brought by Ms Smith, while Mr Singh sought document production against Mr Yeo.*

The second example shows how shorthand that reflects the context of the dispute can be more intuitive to the reader:

> *Accompanied by the 1st Non-Party, the Plaintiff applied for a personal protection order against the Defendant.*

Now compare it with (assume that the various parties had earlier been defined by reference to their familial capacities):

> *Accompanied by Fourth Uncle, Father applied for a personal protection order against Mother.*

Similarly, shorthand can simplify references to multiple charges or claims. Listing them by number ('the 1st, 2nd, 4th, and 8th Charges on the one hand, and the 5th Charge on the other') may be technically precise, but it forces the reader to retain the charge numbering in mind (or, more commonly, to return to the part of the judgment where the charges are enumerated). Grouping the charges under intuitive descriptive labels ('the Harassment Charges' and 'the Theft Charge') helps to convey the meaning precisely.

Finally, shorthand can also be used to organise and label clusters of arguments. This is particularly helpful where the parties advance multiple, overlapping submissions. Grouping them under clear shorthand labels can greatly improve readability and comprehension. An example is *Gillingham James Ian v Fearless Legends Pte Ltd*,[26] where the court synthesised a party's multiple submissions and organised these under nine headings, each assigned a shorthand name (e.g., the 'Circumvention Argument', the 'No Diversion Argument', and the 'No Remedy Argument'). These labels enabled the court to refer to the arguments efficiently and helped the reader follow the analysis without having to revisit the full exposition each time.

When and how should shorthand be used? The touchstone is always whether the selected shorthand makes the judgment easier to read and understand. I suggest the following three-stage approach when thinking about the use of shorthand.

Whether Shorthand Is Warranted

The first stage involves deciding whether shorthand is warranted in the specific instance at hand. Three considerations guide this decision: necessity, proportionality, and frequency.

Necessity asks whether shorthand is needed to aid understanding. If a term is easily understood on its own, shorthand may not enhance clarity. For instance, the 'doctrine of frustration' may not benefit from being abbreviated to 'DOF'. In this regard, I have received submissions where counsel defined the accused person as 'YA' ('your Accused'). Such a shorthand is not necessary to aid understanding, given that a reference to the 'Accused' is easily understood on its own. Acronymising it makes for fragmented reading, and even risks trivialising the solemnity of the proceedings – 'YA was misunderstood' could perhaps pass for a text message or even rap lyrics.

Proportionality looks at the length of the original term. The longer the term, the greater the benefit of shorthand. For instance, using 'CDSA' as shorthand for the 'Corruption, Drug Trafficking And Other Serious Crimes (Confiscation of Benefits) Act' is a proportionate use given the length of the original term; using 'SC' in place of a relatively short 'Supreme Court', less so.

Frequency considers how often the term recurs in the judgment. A term cited once or twice may be better left in full, while one cited many times may benefit from shorthand.

What Form the Shorthand Should Take

If shorthand is warranted, the second stage is choosing what form it should take. Here, three principles are key: intuitiveness, context, and common usage.

The chosen shorthand must be *intuitive* to the reader. 'ROC 2021' for the 'Rules of Court 2021' is clear, whereas 'R21' is not (in Singapore, the latter carries a different connotation altogether).[27] 'SC' for 'Supreme Court' (as discussed earlier in the context of proportionality) could, in Singapore's context, be confused with 'Senior Counsel'. Similarly, 'Harassment Charges' conveys meaning at a glance, while adopting a shorthand of 'Charges 4, 6, 8' obscures rather than clarifies. In addition to being intuitive on its own, different terms should not be given overlapping or confusingly similar shorthand labels (e.g., defining the Rules of Court as 'ROC' and the Registrar of Companies as 'RoC' in the same judgment).

Context also matters. In a family dispute, adopting a shorthand of 'Fourth Uncle' to identify the individual may aid comprehension since he is – well – the fourth uncle in the family hierarchy. But in a commercial dispute within a family-run company, it may be clearer to refer to the person's business role, such as 'Executive Director', even if he is indeed the fourth uncle in the same family structure.

Finally, it is better to adopt shorthand that is already *commonly used*. For instance, in Singapore's context, the Protection from Harassment Act is commonly referred to as 'POHA'.[28] Inventing a new contraction such as 'PFHA', even if it technically accurately represents an acronym of the statute's title, risks confusing readers who expect the established shorthand. Using familiar forms ensures consistency with legal practice and aids comprehension.

Ensuring Consistency

The third stage is ensuring consistency in using the defined shorthand.

Once shorthand is adopted, it should be used throughout the judgment. For instance, if the claimant is defined as 'Father' from the outset of the judgment, it is best to use that shorthand whenever referring to the claimant. Occasionally referring him in other ways (including as 'the claimant') could lead to confusion: was the judge referring to the same person, or to someone else? Likewise, if the Employment Act is defined as 'EA' from the outset, interchangeably referring to 'the Act' could, in some circumstances, lead to confusion.

By maintaining one shorthand per concept and using it consistently throughout the judgment, the judgment minimises ambiguity and enhances precision.

Organising With Lists

Ordered lists – whether numbered or lettered – are useful tools to help organise material, particularly when these relate to statutory tests or multi-limbed standards, procedural stages, or chronological developments.

In *Tan Cheng Bock v Attorney-General*,[29] the Singapore Court of Appeal exemplified this technique in its explanation of purposive statutory interpretation under section 9A of the Interpretation Act. Rather than relying on dense explanatory prose, the court presented the reasoning as a lettered list, coupled with ordinal signposts ('First', 'Second', 'Third'), as follows:

(a) First, ascertain the possible interpretations of the provision, having regard not just to the text of the provision but also to the context of that provision within the written law as a whole.
(b) Second, ascertain the legislative purpose or object of the statute.
(c) Third, compare the possible interpretations of the text against the purposes or objects of the statute.

This ensured clarity by delineating the task at each stage and helped make the reasoning process more easily understood. This specific list presentation has facilitated cross-references in subsequent cases, often in the form of 'Stage [X] of the *Tan Cheng Bock* framework'.[30]

That said, ordered lists should not be overused. A poorly defined list can invite misunderstanding by muddling categories and falsely suggesting that each item bears equal weight. A list of excessive length also risks cognitively overloading the reader, making it difficult for the reader to retain or evaluate the listed items.

The following list, taken from a hypothetical tort case involving a property owner's breach of his duty of care to a visitor who suffered injury as a result, highlights some of these difficulties:

To determine whether the Defendant breached the duty of care, the Court considered the following fifteen factors:

(1) Whether the premises were well-lit;
(2) Whether warning signs were posted;
(3) Whether the floor was dry;
(4) Whether the visitor was wearing appropriate footwear;
(5) Whether the Defendant had conducted regular inspections;
(6) Whether the hazard was visible;
(7) Whether the hazard was temporary or permanent;
(8) Whether the Defendant had knowledge of the hazard;
(9) Whether the visitor was accompanied;
(10) Whether the incident occurred during business hours;
(11) Whether the Defendant had a safety protocol;
(12) Whether the visitor had been previously warned;

(13) *Whether the Defendant offered assistance post-incident;*
(14) *Whether the visitor was familiar with the premises;*
(15) *Whether the Defendant expressed remorse.*

This illustrative list presents multiple difficulties. It suffers from category and doctrinal confusion, conflating factual conditions (e.g., lighting, floor dryness), actor conduct (e.g., inspections, warnings), visitor characteristics (e.g., footwear, familiarity), and post-incident responses (e.g., remorse, assistance). It is unclear whether these factors relate to breach of duty, contributory negligence, mitigation, or damages. The list also creates false equivalence, implying that each factor bears equal weight, when in fact some (e.g., knowledge of the hazard) are central to establishing breach, while others (e.g., remorse) are legally irrelevant to tortious liability. In addition, a 15-factor enumeration risks overwhelming the reader and diluting focus, especially when the factors are not clearly prioritised or grouped.

What about unordered lists (also known as 'bullet points')? These are best reserved for internal notes or preparatory outlines, rather than published written judgments. Internal materials, being provisional, may benefit from fragmentation as a tool of thought (see Chapter 6). They allow the writer to isolate concepts, brainstorm freely, and cluster ideas without committing to a final rhetorical structure. However, in published judgments, unordered lists pose difficulties.

- They encourage fragmentation of tone:
  - Judicial voice thrives on flow. Bullet points interrupt it.
  - Even well-intentioned phrasing can feel clipped or transactional.
- They obscure relational logic even when phrased in complete sentences, they may fail to signal how the points relate to each other:
  - Are the sub-points independent?
    - Or merely illustrative?
    - Or cumulative?
  - Are they exhaustive?
  - The reader shouldn't have to guess.
    - Structure should disclose intent.
    - Unordered lists like this one do not.

- They frustrate citation:
  - How does one cross-refer precisely and concisely to the 'second sub-point of the third bullet in paragraph 45'?

If you find yourself re-reading the above to grasp its structure, to count layers of bullet points, or to figure out how to cross-refer to a specific point in the list, the caution sounded is sufficiently illustrated.

Tabling the Point

Tables offer a useful method for structuring information spatially, allowing the reader to grasp relationships, comparisons, or outcomes at a glance. In certain situations, given their ability to contain detailed content, they may be able to replace prose altogether (unlike graphs, timelines, or diagrams discussed later, which tend to supplement prose). Tables have been used in many judgments, to good effect. Here, I highlight five such use cases drawing from a sampling of Singapore judgments.

First, for mapping parties, roles, and relationships. In multi-party litigation, tables can usefully clarify who is involved in a case, how they are connected, and what roles they play. For example, in *Public Prosecutor v Soh Chee Wen*,[31] a highly complex case relating to stock market manipulation that resulted in a judgment of almost 900 pages excluding appendices, the Singapore High Court used a glossary-style table to summarise the individuals and corporations, their roles, whether they gave evidence, and cross-references to trial documents.[32]

Second, for conveying evidential detail across a chronological frame particularly where the court had to track developments over time and correlate them with specific facts. In *Ayaz Ahmad v Mustaq Ahmad @ Mushtaq Ahmad s/o Mustafa*,[33] one of the issues was whether the defendants had acted oppressively by causing or allowing the family-owned company to withhold payment of shareholder dividends while paying the defendants substantial directors' fees. The court deployed a table to synthesise a timeline of key events alongside evidence on directors' fees and dividend declarations.[34]

Third, for summarising legal issues, outcomes, and parties' positions. Tables can distil complex holdings by listing issues, grounds of appeal, and the court's decision on each. For example, in *Aljunied-Hougang Town Council v Lim Swee Lian Sylvia*,[35] the Singapore High Court utilised a table to summarise key findings on liability in respect of the defendants, as well as the remedies which the plaintiffs may pursue against the defendants in respect of the claims for which liability was found.[36] On appeal to the Singapore Court of Appeal, the appellate court reproduced one of the Singapore High Court's tables, and also set out a table outlining the parties involved in the suits and the respective appeals.[37] In *Parakou Investment Holdings Pte Ltd v Parakou Shipping Pte Ltd (in liquidation)*,[38] the Singapore Court of Appeal used a table to summarise the 11 grounds of appeal and the court's decision on each issue.[39] The court also included a table in an annex, summarising the orders made against each of the defendants.[40] In *Foo Jee Seng v Foo Jhee Tuang*,[41] the Singapore High Court included a table showing each beneficiary's percentage interest in the property and their position on its sale,[42] supporting the conclusion that the majority favoured sale.

Fourth, for setting out voluminous data. In fact-heavy cases, tables can help organise large quantities of information. In *Public Prosecutor v Soh Chee Wen*,[43] the judgment included a Microsoft Excel workbook containing linked worksheets that tabulated charges, account details, and signatories across 189 trading accounts.

Fifth, for summarising the law as applied to different scenarios or archetypal situations. In *RDC Concrete Pte Ltd v Sato Kogyo (S) Pte Ltd*,[44] the Singapore Court of Appeal summarised the situations entitling an innocent party to terminate a contract at common law by setting out the various scenarios in a table. One can compare the utility of the table with the text equivalent of the summary found in *Man Financial (S) Pte Ltd v Wong Bark Chuan David*.[45]

Speaking a Thousand Words

While visual tools and aids were once rare in written judgments, their use has grown markedly in recent years. This has no doubt been driven in part by technological advances that make such aids easier to create, embed, and share. But the shift is not merely technical. It reflects a deeper recognition that clarity is not always best served by prose alone. As legal disputes become more intricate and data-rich, visualisation offers a way to manage complexity without sacrificing concision and precision. Properly deployed visual aids can enhance comprehension and reinforce judicial reasoning. As the adage reminds us, a picture is (sometimes) worth a thousand words. Here, I explore three types of visual tools: graphs, timelines, and diagrams.

Graphs can offer insight by highlighting trends, relationships, or shifts that prose alone may struggle to explain. For instance, in *Vasentha d/o Joseph v Public Prosecutor*,[46] the Singapore High Court used a scatter plot graph to test the prosecution's submission that case law shows a correlation between the quantity of diamorphine trafficked and the length of the imprisonment term imposed.[47] This allowed the court to explain that there was no clear correlation, apart from a general upward trend.

Timelines can make procedural history or chronology easier to follow. For instance, in *Goh Guan Sin (by her litigation representative Chiam Yu Zhu) v Yeo Tseng Tsai*,[48] the Singapore High Court presented a timeline of the key changes in the plaintiff's neurological parameters in the form of a line graph to illustrate the deterioration of her condition in the hours after her surgery.[49]

Diagrams can convey conceptual relationships more intuitively than paragraphs of explanation. For instance, in *Love & Co Pte Ltd v The Carat Club Pte Ltd*,[50] the Singapore High Court used a Venn diagram to illustrate the absolute grounds for refusing the registration of trade marks under specific provisions of the Trade Marks Act,[51] followed by prose to help the reader better understand the conceptual lay of the land. In *L Capital Jones Ltd v Maniach Pte Ltd*,[52] *DNZ v DOA*,[53] and *Hyatt Terminal and Industrial Corp v Filipinas Third Millenium Realty Corp*,[54] the Singapore Court of Appeal and the Singapore International Commercial Court employed flowchart diagrams to illustrate corporate ownership and control structures.[55] In *Foo Jee Seng v Foo Jhee Tuang*,[56] the Singapore Court of Appeal utilised a diagram to detail the members of a family and the respective roles they played in the proceedings.

For completeness, there have been critiques of certain decisions where the lower court utilised visualisation in relation to sentencing frameworks or benchmarks. These critiques, however, did not take issue with the use of visual tools as aids to facilitate understanding. Rather, the critiques were directed at the underlying analytical approach (which were, to be sure, accurately represented in the visuals). For instance, in *Syed Fathuddin Putra bin Syed A Rahman v Public Prosecutor*, the Singapore Court of Appeal observed that the use of a graph in depicting the sentencing framework and benchmarks for criminal offences gave the 'semblance of predictability and precision' which may come 'at the expense of judgment and consideration of circumstances'.[57] In *Public Prosecutor v Takaaki Masui*,[58] the Singapore Court of Appeal disagreed with an 'excessively complex or technical sentencing framework[s]'[59] which involved the use of a three-dimensional model to visualise a 'double variable sentencing framework'.[60]

The upshot is that when the underlying framework is sound, visualisation can enhance precision and concision; but when there are issues with the underlying framework, visualisation cannot redeem it.

CONCLUDING REFLECTIONS

A boardgame's rulebook does not simplify the game by compromising its depth. Rather, it organises complexity through concision and precision, allowing players to grasp the rules swiftly and navigate the game with confidence.

Soon after reading the *Nanty Narking* manual, my family was engrossed in exploring this 'truly Victorian game of wit and podsnappery'.[61] Within a few weekends, we had become adept at it. Wonderful family bonding moments over a beautifully designed board were made possible by a few pages of well-written instructions and visual aids.

Judicial writing, at its best, performs a similar function: it guides the reader through the reasoning with concision and precision. The techniques explored in this chapter do not aim to make judgments shorter or simpler for their own sake. Used well, these techniques can help illuminate judicial reasoning in service of justice. Precise and concise judicial writing gets to the point and helps the reader to get there too.

NOTES

1 Many of these are available on YouTube.

2 Steven D Stark, *Writing to Win: The Legal Writer* (2nd edn, Three Rivers Press 2012) 232.

3 In a different context, Justice Phang has made a similar point: see Andrew Phang, 'Litigation in Appellate Courts' (2024) 36 SAcLJ 617, 618, where he said, referring to his approach in that article 'it is hoped that, whilst simple, it will not be perceived as being simplistic'.

4 See e.g. Richard C Wydick, *Plain English for Lawyers* (5th edn, Carolina Academic Press 2005).

5 Bo Seo, *Good Arguments: How Debate Teaches Us to Listen and Be Heard* (Penguin Press 2022) 136.

6 Godfrey Cole and others, *Making Decisions Judicially: A Guide for Decision-Makers* (Hart Publishing 2022) 163.

7 See the discussion in Chapter 1 (on 'Affirming Participation and Respect').

8 From 2003 to 2023.

9 Lim How Khang, 'An Empirical Study on Judgments Written by the Supreme Court Judges of Singapore' (*Singapore Courts*, 2025) <https://perma.cc/P5KZ-2YJ7> 31.

10 See e.g. Ken Hyland, 'Metadiscourse: What Is It and Where Is It Going?' (2017) 113 J Pragmat 16.

11 Joseph Williams and Joseph Bizup, *Style: The Basics of Clarity and Grace* (11th edn, Pearson 2013) 75.

12 I am alive to the irony that 'etc.' is in fact a Latin abbreviation, being short for the Latin phrase *et cetera*.

13 See e.g. Wydick (n 4).

14 For instance, Singapore's Rules of Court 2021 has replaced some Latin phrases with English equivalents (for instance, '*amicus curiae*' is now 'independent counsel', '*in camera*' is 'in private', etc.), while other less-familiar English phrases are now replaced with

simplified equivalents (for instance, 'leave' is now 'permission', 'deposition' is now 'pre-trial examination', etc.): see Singapore Courts, 'Digest 1: General Overview of the New Rules of Court – What Is New?' <https://perma.cc/Q327-7YTC>. There is also an initiative known as 'Plain Laws Understandable by Singaporeans' (acronymised as 'PLUS') by the Legislation Division of Singapore's Attorney-General's Chambers: Attorney-General's Chambers, 'Plain Laws Understandable by Singaporeans' (27 June 2025) <https://perma.cc/VN4S-97JV>.

15 See e.g. the Singapore Academy of Law's 'Plain English for Latin Expressions' at Law Reform Committee, Singapore Academy of Law, 'Plain English for Latin Expressions' <https://perma.cc/A29V-HRYV>.

16 Edward Berry, *Writing Reasons: A Handbook for Judges* (6th edn, LexisNexis Canada 2025) 87.

17 See e.g. the use of plain language in *Public Prosecutor v GMS Carwerkz* [2026] SGMC 15 [37], explaining that *mens rea* is 'the requirement that an accused person must have acted with the requisite mental state before being convicted for a criminal offence'.

18 Berry (n 16) 83.

19 Natalie Skead and Justin Yeo, 'Judicial Education in a Brave New World' (2025) 59 Law Teach 666, 668.

20 [2023] SGCA 5, [2023] 1 SLR 987.

21 The 'Technology Tutorial' took place over three half-days. It involved experts addressing the court to assist the court in understanding the highly complex technical issues at play in a patent dispute.

22 [2020] SGCA(I) 2, [2020] 2 SLR 20.

23 Paul Loy and Asher Chin, 'Singapore Continues to Develop Protections for Crypto Assets Holders' (*IFC Review*, 9 August 2023) <https://perma.cc/59JG-TSXQ>; Jonathan Crompton, 'Singapore Court of Appeal Issues Landmark Decision in First Cryptocurrency Related Trial' (*Reynolds Porter Chamberlain LLP*, 9 June 2021) <https://perma.cc/Y9C7-7CYF>; Selina Lum, 'Bitcoin Trial: Apex Court Finds Virtual Currency Exchange Operator in Breach of Contract' *The Straits Times* (24 February 2020) <https://perma.cc/JVN3-U62H>.

24 This touches on both the first and second types of complexity mentioned earlier, that is, complexity arising from the expanding scope of scientific and technological knowledge required to resolve disputes, and complexity arising from novel issues that challenge the understanding and application of existing legal principles.

25 *Quoine* (n 22) 15.

26 [2023] SGHCR 13 [8] to [10]. Note that the reported version of the judgment ([2024] 6 SLR 697) is limited only to selected issues and does not include the court's synthesis of arguments. This case is also mentioned in Chapter 2, n 15.

27 In Singapore, 'R21' is a film classification that refers to 'Restricted 21'. Such films are restricted to persons aged 21 and above.

28 Indeed, it is also referred to as 'POHA' in government bills referring to the Protection from Harassment Act, although not within the Protection from Harassment Act itself.

29 [2017] SGCA 50, [2017] 2 SLR 850 [37].

30 See e.g. *Imran bin Mohd Arip v Public Prosecutor* [2021] SGCA 91, [2021] 2 SLR 1198 [70]–[89].

31 [2023] SGHC 299.

32 *Soh Chee Wen* (n 31) Appendix 2.

33 [2022] SGHC 241.

34 *Ayaz Ahmad* (n 33) 516.

35 [2019] SGHC 241.

36 *Aljunied-Hougang Town Council* (n 35) 447, 643.

37 *How Weng Fan v Sengkang Town Council* [2022] SGCA 72, [2023] 1 SLR 707 [99], Annex.

38 [2018] SGCA 3, [2018] 1 SLR 271.

39 *Parakou* (n 38) 37.

40 *Parakou* (n 38) 133, Annex 2.

41 [2012] SGCA 41, [2012] 4 SLR 339.

42 *Foo Jee Seng* (n 41) 65.

43 *Soh Chee Wen* (n 31) 1495, Appendix 2.

44 [2007] SGCA 39, [2007] 4 SLR(R) 413 [113].

45 [2007] SGCA 53, [2008] 1 SLR(R) 663 [153]–[158].

46 [2015] SGHC 197, [2015] 5 SLR 122.

47 *Vasentha* (n 46) 29.

48 [2019] SGHC 274, [2021] 3 SLR 364 [168].

49 *Goh Guan Sin* (n 48) 168.

50 [2008] SGHC 158, [2009] 1 SLR(R) 561.

51 *The Carat Club* (n 50) 49, Annex A.

52 [2017] SGCA 3, [2017] 1 SLR 312.

53 [2026] SGHC(I) 1 [4].

54 [2026] SGHC(I) 3 [9].

55 *L Capital Jones* (n 52) 4.

56 *Foo Jee Seng* (n 41) 2.

57 See *Syed Fathuddin Putra bin Syed A Rahman v Public Prosecutor* [2023] SGHC 338, [2024] 3 SLR 1672 [37]–[38], where the Court agreed with the observations in *Ripon v Public Prosecutor* [2022] SGHC 255, [2023] 3 SLR 896 [7], which critiqued the use of a graphical sentencing framework in *Public Prosecutor v Pang Shuo* [2016] SGHC 82, [2016] 3 SLR 903.

58 [2021] SGCA 119, [2022] 1 SLR 1033.

59 *Takaaki Masui* (n 58) 14, 15.

60 *Takaaki Masui v Public Prosecutor* [2020] SGHC 265, [2021] 4 SLR 160 [129].

61 This is the tagline of *Nanty Narking*. The term 'podsnappery' is a neologism (that is, literary coinage), drawn from the character Mr Podsnap in Charles Dickens' novel *Our Mutual Friend*, referencing 'an attitude toward life marked by complacency and a refusal to recognize unpleasant facts': see 'Podsnappery' (*Merriam-Webster Dictionary*) <https://perma.cc/3Z8P-H8KU>.

A Judicious Tone – Writing with Respect and Humility

Five

Early in my judicial career, I heard an application for discovery against a non-party to the proceedings. In gist, an anonymous person had posted on an online bulletin board under the moniker 'Zorro' – a name popularised by the famous fictional American masked vigilante. The party seeking discovery asked the court to compel the non-party's disclosure of that person's identity. After hearing the arguments, I granted the application. At that time, it crossed my mind to refer to this in my judgment as the 'unmasking of Zorro'. It would have been clever, perhaps even memorable. I might well have garnered a few laughs, or even been cited by the media (or on social media).

But it would also have been inappropriate. The judgment was neither about me nor my penchant for levity. It was a public act of reasoning, delivered in the voice of the court. However well the circumstances lent themselves to wit and wordplay, the parties were entitled to a judgment that treated their dispute with seriousness, and that sounded as such. The court's role was not to entertain but to adjudicate.

That moment reminded me that in each judgment, it is not just *what* the judge says that matters but also *how* the judge says it. A decision may be correct in law and meticulous in reasoning yet still falter in how it is received because of the tone it employs. Tone is not merely a matter of style. It is a form of expression and a reflection of the act of judgment itself. It reveals how the court sees its role, and how it regards those who stand before it. It does not simply wrap the reasoning – it is *part* of it. It shapes how the court's decision is formed, framed, and felt.

This chapter explores the judicial tone from two complementary perspectives: *respect* and *humility*. Respect relates to the court's outward posture – how it addresses parties, counsel, other courts, and the broader readership of its judgments. Humility relates to its inward posture – how it conceives of its own authority and its limits. One regulates how the court speaks to others; the other regulates how it speaks of itself.

DOI: 10.4324/9781042017027-6

Together, they ensure that the judicial voice remains measured, principled, and worthy of the authority it wields.

RESPECT

Respect governs how the court addresses others. Writing with respect means giving the judgment an appropriate institutional tone – one that avoids overly casual turns of phrase, that disagrees without disparaging, and that avoids sarcasm or ridicule.

Avoiding Overly Casual Turns of Phrase

Judgments must retain a formal register. Such formality communicates the seriousness of the subject matter. It signals that the court's words are institutional and deliberative, not personal or impulsive.

Colloquial and casual phrasing may seem innocuous – or even engaging, accessible, and conversational. Indeed, I have had conversations with judges who thought that colloquial language can help enhance the accessibility of their judgments. As against this, it is important to ensure that casual phrasing does not inadvertently make judicial reasoning sound like an informal opinion or suggest that a judgment is driven by personal impression rather than objective analysis.

Contrast the tonal shift in the following examples:

> *The defendant's story was a hot mess. → The defendant's account was inconsistent and lacked credibility.*

> *The company messed up big time. → The company committed significant breaches of its obligations.*

> *Defence counsel tried to pull a fast one. → Defence counsel advanced a misleading argument.*

Unlike the initial formulations, the alternative formulations are formal and legally grounded. They identify the nature of the problem and its consequence in terms that are meaningful within the judicial process. They add a semblance of composure and authority to the written decision.

Some casual language may even undermine confidence in the judgment. Contrast the tonal shift in the following examples:

> *To be honest, that was not a good reason.* → *The justification offered was insufficient and unconvincing.*

> *Frankly speaking, I found it hard to believe the witness.* → *The witness's testimony was implausible and lacked credibility.*

Phrases such as 'to be honest' or 'frankly speaking' are unexceptional in everyday conversation but may not be the most suitable for written judgments. The presence of these phrases may inadvertently suggest that the judge's candour is occasional rather than constant. They may also frame the judge's assessment as a personal opinion rather than an institutional evaluation.

Respectful judicial writing avoids overly casual language as deliberately as it avoids elevated or grandiose phrasing.[1] What is needed is a tone that is measured, balanced, and in plain language. Written judgments are public documents, read by parties, the profession, the press, and the public.[2] A formal register ensures that the judgment speaks across these audiences, including international audiences, with respect.

Disagreeing Without Disparaging

One face of judicial respect is revealed in moments of departure, that is, when a court disagrees with the reasoning or conclusion of another court, whether coordinate, lower, or foreign. These divergences are features, not bugs, of the common law method. They are integral to the common law's dialogic evolution.

Yet, the manner in which they are expressed matters deeply. A disagreement should be marked by grace, not bravado; by institutional civility, not an air of conquest. The goal is not to assert superiority of intellect, hierarchy, or jurisdiction, but to respectfully explain the reasons for the divergence. A judgment that sounds dismissive or condescending does more than fray professional courtesy; it risks weakening the court's perceived neutrality and the broader judicial fabric.

Contrast the tonal shift in the following examples:

> *The interpretation adopted by Judge X reflects a troubling departure from established principles and serves only to erode doctrinal clarity.* → *I respectfully reach a different conclusion from ABC v XYZ. For the following reasons, Interpretation A more closely aligns with established principles.*

Each expresses disagreement, but the difference in tone is marked. The first targets a named judge[3] with critical force and rhetorical dominance, casting the court's voice in an adversarial light. The second speaks from within the institutional tradition, its disagreement shaped by respect rather than rebuke. It exemplifies a mode of departure that sustains collegiality and encourages reflection on what the law is (or ought to be).

It may help to think of judicial reasoning not as solitary assertion, but as one voice within an ongoing conversation. After all, the common law is a tradition that thrives on a principled exchange of ideas. In this way, the law's evolution is sustained by judgments that disagree without disparaging.

Refraining From Sarcasm or Ridicule

Another face of respect is revealed in how the court characterises the arguments before it. A judgment that mocks or belittles a party risks sounding less like an institutional pronouncement and more like a polemic.[4]

Contrast the tonal shift in the following examples:

> *Witness X must have thought the oath was a mere formality.* → *Witness X's testimony was inconsistent with the oath he had taken to speak only the truth.*

> *Counsel proceeded as if the cited precedents were optional.* → *Counsel's submission did not engage with the cited precedents.*

Each pair conveys a similar substantive assessment, but the tone diverges sharply. Sarcasm stings, suggesting that the party or counsel is foolish or insincere. Ridicule openly mocks the argument (or worse, the arguer) as laughable or absurd. Both diminish the dignity of the judgment and risk casting the court as partisan or impatient. By contrast, the restrained formulations identify the flaw directly, in terms that are legally meaningful and institutionally respectful.

Sarcasm and ridicule also carry unintended consequences. They are often picked up by the media and can overshadow the court's substantive reasoning.[5] They may sometimes invite doubt about the court's impartiality, suggesting irritation or bias rather than principled analysis.

HUMILITY

In addition to being respectful, judgments must also reflect judicial humility. In this book, I use this term to refer to an inward posture – how the court conceives of its own authority and its limits. Judicial humility in judgment writing requires wisdom in emotional expression, rhetorical choice, and doctrinal scope. The degree of latitude may vary across judicial levels and cultures, but humility remains a constant touchstone.

Emotional Expression

Humility in emotional expression ensures that the court's voice reflects its institutional role, rather than the personal emotional reactions of the judge. While this does not require the judge to be completely detached or unfeeling, it does require that the court's voice remain measured and grounded in evidence rather than personal sentiment. The aim is not to purge judgments of humanity, but to ensure that expressions of empathy or moral clarity serve the reasoning rather than eclipsing it.

Excessively emotional phrasing can suggest bias, personal investment in the outcome, or an attempt to sway through emotion rather than reason. The difference lies not in *whether* emotion is acknowledged, but in *how* it is expressed. Even in the context of competitive debating, caution has been sounded against 'emoting' – 'a performance in which emotions no longer correspond to the situation at hand'.[6] Even more so, then, in the context of judgment writing, where the court's voice must be anchored in principled reasoning rather than emotional display.

Consider the following illustration.

> *The mother was shattered by grief so unbearable, even I struggled to fathom its depth. → The nature and extent of the mother's emotional suffering are evident from the evidence before the court.*

The first sentence is emotive and dramatic. It signals the judge's immersion in one party's experience and risks shifting the judicial voice toward advocacy or personal sentiment. The second is measured and appropriate for a judgment: it acknowledges the gravity of the mother's suffering while anchoring that recognition in the evidence.

As another illustration:

> *I was deeply moved by Mr X's heartfelt testimony – it was a rare moment of raw truth that stirred even the most seasoned observers in the courtroom.* → *Mr X demonstrated sincerity and credibility on the stand.*

The first sentence immerses the judge in the emotional response, using collective sentiment to elevate the witness's testimony. The second comes across more impartial and focused by acknowledging the witness's qualities in legally relevant terms.

These examples underscore that judges should be careful when using language steeped in overt emotionality. That said, judgments need not be devoid of compassion, for dispassion does not mean indifference. There may be moments where the court's empathy is appropriately expressed when acknowledging human pain or dignity. Appropriately deployed, such expression is consistent with the court's institutional role.

One excellent example of this is found in *Public Prosecutor v Gaiyathiri d/o Murugayan*.[7] This was a horrific case of abuse of a foreign domestic worker. The victim had been kicked, stomped, dragged across the floor by her hair, and had lost 14 kg during the 14 months of her employment, weighing only 24 kg at the time of her demise. In the judgment, the Singapore High Court counselled caution on emotiveness:[8]

> *The court should of course not shy away from conveying the strongest disapprobation of offending conduct and expressing outrage on behalf of society in appropriate cases such as this. But emotiveness can impede full and fair consideration of all relevant factors.*

While the last sentence of that quote was directed at the process of deciding the appropriate sentence, the same principle applies with equal force to the language and tone used to convey that decision.

The court went on to express strong disapprobation of abhorrent behaviour in the following way:[9]

> The cruel and inhumane methods that the Accused had chosen to employ in order to punish the Deceased were conscious and deliberate. They reflected an utter lack of any basic humanity. The Prosecution submitted that the Accused had treated the Deceased as a lesser human being. In my assessment, what the Accused had done to the Deceased demonstrated that she had callously regarded the Deceased as even less than a human being. In her final hours, the Deceased was kicked, strangled, pulled by her hair, stomped upon and punched like a punching bag or some inanimate object. In the 35 days leading up to her death, she had endured repeated assaults, including being lifted and dragged by her hair and being spun round like a rag doll by the Accused. This much was incontrovertibly revealed from the CCTV footage alone. The Deceased was defenceless. She was at the total mercy of the Accused. The Accused showed no mercy whatsoever.

This passage exemplifies the kind of disciplined disapprobation a judge must sometimes voice – forceful in its moral clarity, yet free of theatricality. Here, the judge used phrases like 'utter lack of any basic humanity' and 'even less than a human being'. These are unequivocally condemnatory, but completely appropriate in the context and proportionate to the gravity of the conduct described. The metaphors ('rag doll', 'punching bag') are vivid, but not gratuitous. They serve to clarify the dehumanisation that the victim suffered. Throughout the extract, the judge's voice remains firmly within the bounds of what society expects from its courts: that it speaks not from personal emotion, but for justice.

In cases such as *Gaiyathiri*, the judge faces a difficult dual imperative: to give voice to society's moral outrage, while safeguarding the clarity and composure befitting the judicial office. The preceding extract illustrates that this balance is not only possible but, when skilfully done, is also powerful and persuasive.

Rhetorical Choice

Humility in rhetorical choice concerns the style and ornament of judicial expression. Wit, flourish, or sensational detail may enliven prose, but they also carry risks: they can distract from the reasoning, invite misunderstanding, or diminish the seriousness of the dispute. Judicial humility therefore calls for a measured voice, ensuring that rhetorical devices serve the court's reasoning, rather than overshadow it. This includes an awareness that rhetorical effects are not culturally neutral: a metaphor that resonates in one community may fall flat – or even misfire – in another, and humour that feels well pitched to one reader may feel inappropriate or jarring to another. In what follows, I focus on three specific areas: sensationalism, metaphors and analogies, and humour and wit.

Sensationalism

Judges should resist the temptation to 'play to the gallery' through sensationalising the case before them. This applies during the actual hearing of the case but also in the written judgment that ensues. Formulations that unnecessarily dramatise the dispute may appeal to headline writers but add little to judicial authority or stature.

Sensational language may offend parties who feel that their private lives have been turned into spectacle. It may compound trauma to vulnerable litigants or witnesses who feel exploited rather than respected. Sensational writing may also distort public understanding of the case, leading the public to focus attention on lurid details rather than the court's reasoning.

Contrast the tonal shift in the following examples:

> *The defendant's actions unleashed a sordid tale of betrayal and deceit. → The defendant's conduct involved breaches of trust and misrepresentation.*

> *The defendant orchestrated a chilling spectacle of fraud. → The defendant engaged in fraudulent conduct involving multiple fraudulent misrepresentations.*

Both examples show how sensational phrasing dramatises the dispute, while the alternative formulations ground it in legal analysis. The first formulation in each pair casts the case in a register that may gratify headline writers but risks trivialising the seriousness of the dispute and shifting attention from the court's reasoning to its rhetoric. By contrast, the second formulation identifies the precise nature of the wrongdoing in legally meaningful terms.

As a general guideline, it is advisable to avoid theatrical verbs (e.g., 'orchestrated', 'unleashed'), adjectives (e.g., 'sordid', 'chilling'), and nouns (e.g., 'spectacle', 'drama') unless these are genuinely required by the circumstances of the case – for instance, to justifiably express the gravity of the conduct, the vulnerability of a party, or the seriousness of the harm. In most situations, precise legal terminology or neutral phrasing serve as guardrails against lapsing into sensationalism.

Metaphor and Analogy

Another dimension of rhetorical discipline concerns the use of metaphor and analogy. Judges sometimes reach for these devices to clarify complex ideas, and when used with care, they can greatly aid understanding. Judicial humility does not require the avoidance of such devices. Rather, it requires that judges use metaphors and analogies carefully to serve judicial reasoning.

Metaphors and analogies are related but distinct concepts. Analogies assert that 'this thing is like that thing' and thus should be treated similarly, whereas metaphors draw a comparison between the thing being described (known as the 'tenor') and the thing doing the describing (known as the 'vehicle') without asserting that they are alike.[10]

Analogies are common in legal discourse and an accepted part of legal analysis.[11] When drawn from legally and factually comparable contexts, they are a key tool for developing the law and strengthening doctrine. Indeed, analogical reasoning lies at the heart of the common law's doctrine of precedent, enabling courts to extend principles from one situation to another in a principled way.

In *Donoghue v Stevenson*, perhaps the most famous common law decision,[12] Lord Atkin drew upon earlier authorities that recognised duties of care in particular relationships – cases involving 'some general conception of relations giving rise to a duty of care'.[13] He reasoned by analogy that a manufacturer of a sealed bottle (of ginger beer, which contained a decomposed snail) owed a similar duty to the ultimate consumer. In doing so, he laid the foundation of the modern law of negligence.[14]

But what is most memorable about Lord Atkin's decision is not the analogies to past cases and similar factual situations, but his articulation of the 'neighbour principle' – a *metaphor*[15] that underpinned his analogical reasoning. In Lord Atkin's seminal words:[16]

> The rule that you are to love your neighbour becomes in law, you must not injure your neighbour; and the lawyer's question, *Who is my neighbour?* receives a restricted reply. You must take reasonable care to avoid acts or omissions which you can reasonably foresee would be likely to injure your neighbour. *Who, then, in law is my neighbour?* The answer seems to be persons who are so closely and directly affected by my act that I ought reasonably to have them in contemplation as being so affected when I am directing my mind to the acts or omissions which are called in question.

The 'tenor' in this case was the class of persons to whom a duty of care is owed, while the 'vehicle' was the familiar concept of a neighbour.

Although drawn from a Biblical parable (a parable being itself a type of metaphor),[17] Lord Atkin's 'neighbour principle' is understandable even for those not of the Christian faith, since it conveys the idea of proximity and relational responsibility. 'Neighbour' brings to mind norms commonly associated with responsible neighbourliness in the literal sense (i.e., obligations towards the person living next door), but the metaphor extended these normative expectations to relationships of 'non-literal proximity',[18] as was the situation in *Donoghue v Stevenson* itself. One wonders how modern negligence law would have developed had Lord Atkin chosen the less appropriate metaphors of 'friend', 'family', or 'parishioner' instead.

Metaphors are both illuminating and memorable, as the 'neighbour principle' has shown us. They facilitate understanding because they use language appropriate for one (often relatable) thing to draw a comparison to another (often more abstract or less relatable) thing.[19] Common metaphors encountered in the common law include that of the 'fishing expedition' in document discovery,[20] or the 'man on the Clapham omnibus' who represents the hypothetical ordinary and relatable commuter on a London bus.[21] We have also heard of how 'the state of a man's mind is as much a fact as the state of his digestion' (capturing the idea that mental states are factual matters).[22] We may even have encountered sporting metaphors – such as a golfing metaphor that demolished a rigid doctrine of presumed intent ('no-one but a lawyer would say that I must be presumed to have intended to put my ball in the bunker, because that was the natural and probable result of my shot'),[23] or a tennis metaphor to explain the issue of evidential advantage in the context of legal presumptions ('the party in whose favour it falls "starts with advantage of service, it does not also start fifteen or thirty love up"').[24] Indeed, it has been said:[25]

> *We live in a magical world of law where liens float, corporations reside, minds hold meetings, and promises run with the land. The constitutional landscape is dotted with streams, walls, and poisonous trees. And these wonderful things are cradled in the seamless web of law.*

The persuasive and explanatory strength in metaphors also shapes the way we think of concepts.[26] This means that they have the potential to influence doctrine and drive legal development. They can certainly be utilised to excellent effect. But judges ought to use them with care, for as Lord Mansfield warned: 'nothing in law is so apt to mislead as a metaphor'.[27] Or as Judge Cardozo cautioned: '[m]etaphors in law are to be narrowly watched, for starting as devices to liberate thought, they end often by enslaving it' (note, somewhat paradoxically, the use of an enslavement metaphor in this quote).[28]

Humour and Wit

In some cultures and jurisdictions, occasional flashes of judicial humour and wit are commonplace and considered an important part of connecting judges to the public. On one view, humour is a 'quintessentially human quality' that promotes open justice by 'demystifying the language and rituals of the courtroom', 'oil[ing] the wheels of justice by easing courtroom tensions', and 'aiding digestion of complex written reasons'.[29] Some have also argued that humour can help demystify the law, crystallise points, and humanise a case.[30]

One of the key proponents of the use of judicial humour, Judge Irving Goldberg,[31] is reported to have preached:[32]

> Use wit, humor, allusions to history and literature, metaphors and similes. Use verbs. Make an opinion talk. Heck, make it walk.

Walking his talk, in a judgment involving Kentucky Fried Chicken Corp and a packaging company, Judge Goldberg wrote:[33]

> This case presents us with something mundane, something novel, and something bizarre. . . . [T]he bizarre element is the facially implausible – some might say unappetizing – contention that the man whose chicken is 'finger-lickin' good' has unclean hands.

And in a case involving the tax treatment of a shareholder's voluntary surrender of a portion of shares to the corporation, he penned:[34]

> And when a marriage made in heaven plummets to earth, the postlapsarian ceremonies are presided over by that most fallen of angels, the Commissioner of Internal Revenue.

Judge Goldberg is not the only memorable judicial humourist. There are far more to be found in the various sources footnoted at the end of this sentence.[35] In these sources one will find uses of humorous images,[36] headings,[37] entire opinions in rhyme[38] or rap,[39] and the use of pop-culture references.

Humour and wit must be carefully used. Judicial humility reminds the judge that the courtroom is not a stage and that the judgment is not a platform for personal performance, or even a weapon. Humour and wit are also not culturally uniform: what one community receives as light-hearted may strike another as flippant or disrespectful. Expressions of judicial humour and wit must therefore be culturally sensitive, calibrated not only to the subject matter but also to the expectations of the diverse audiences who may encounter the judgment.

It has long been cautioned that humour in judgments can offend, distract, or diminish the perceived seriousness of the court.[40] It may fail to show the parties the proper respect and may cause readers to question if the court had taken its judicial duties seriously.[41] Indeed, there are cautionary tales. In a criminal case, an appellate judge wrote a special concurrence to distance himself from a majority opinion, because he did not believe that humour had a place in a judgment that affected the rights, obligations, and liberty of citizens: 'The case certainly is not funny to the litigants. I concur in the judgment only'.[42] In another case, the use of judicial humour drew heavy criticism. After describing a man's romantic entanglements with three women, a judge remarked that the man's conduct was 'consistent with his apparent success as a used car salesman'.[43] This escalated into a demand for a 'big apology' for denigrating used car salespeople.[44] Nearly a decade later, when delivering a speech to new judges, the same judge advised his audience to be cautious with humour, noting the many cases where 'flippant behaviour has caused unintended but deep offence'.[45]

None of the aforementioned is to suggest that the use of humour or wit is prohibited in judgments. Rather, the point is that humour and wit must not come at the expense of the parties or the dignity of the judicial process.

Doctrinal Scope

Humility in doctrinal scope recognises the limits of the court's role within its legal tradition. In the common law, that authority is exercised within a system shaped by precedent, argument, and adversarial process. It is the adversarial method that sharpens the issues and invites the judge to address only those questions placed before the court. The tensions generated by the parties' arguments help refine the court's answer to the legal question at hand.

In the context of doctrinal scope, humility means deciding only what is necessary to resolve the dispute and resisting the temptation to pronounce broadly, speculate, or generalise beyond the case. Judges learn only what emerges from the evidence and arguments tendered in proceedings; their view of the case is but a 'partial glimpse' of reality.[46] As Chief Justice of Australia Murray Gleeson has cautioned, it may be unfair for a judge to 'express unnecessary value judgments, or opinions, or general conclusions of fact, without knowing the whole of the background in question'.[47] Chief Justice Sundaresh Menon has also cautioned judges against unnecessarily laying down overarching pronouncements, such as by extending a principle beyond what is necessary to dispose of the case at hand.[48] Such wisdom rests on a deeper intellectual humility: the recognition, as Justice Andrew Phang has observed, that as a sitting judge 'there is always something new or more that can be learnt' whether in the law or beyond it.[49] Recognising this helps guard against the temptation to overstate, overreach, or pronounce beyond what the case requires.

The manner in which humility is expressed in relation to doctrinal scope varies across judicial levels. Trial courts should ordinarily confine themselves to the issues as framed by the parties as well as the evidence before them. In contrast, appellate and apex courts may sometimes be required to articulate broader principles or clarify doctrine for future application; but even so, any such broader articulation should remain anchored in the case, the doctrine, and the court's institutional role, rather than in unbounded commentary about society at large.

Humility in doctrinal scope guards against the judicial voice sounding like that of an omniscient oracle. Contrast the following pair of examples:

This case reveals the broader collapse of corporate ethics in modern society. → *This case turns on whether the defendant breached its contractual obligations under the agreement in question.*

This dispute shows that family law is fundamentally broken and in need of reform. → *This dispute highlights the difficulties that arise when custody arrangements are not clearly defined in law.*

The prior examples illustrate that when a court pronounces in sweeping terms about society, morality, or human behaviour, it risks stepping beyond adjudication into social commentary. Such pronouncements are often reported or amplified by the media (or social media), but when they exceed the bounds of the case or are stated without proper substantiation, they blur the distinction between judicial reasoning and public discourse. Humility requires that the court's words remain proportionate to its role in each case and cognisant of the boundaries of its authority.

To be sure, humility does not forbid the court from speaking more broadly when the law itself requires it. In criminal sentencing, for instance, deterrence is a recognised principle. The court must sometimes highlight the prevalence of scams, drug offences, or corruption in explaining its decision to impose a lengthy custodial sentence. These pronouncements are not social commentary for its own sake, but factually and doctrinally anchored statements tied to statutory principles or precedential guidance. The key is to tether any broader observations to the case and to the court's role. For instance, a judgment that says 'deterrence must be the dominant sentencing consideration in this case, given the rising incidence of scams' is justified; one that declares 'as scams are ruining the moral fabric of society, offenders must be severely punished' less so.

In the end, humility in doctrinal scope is about exercising the court's authority within its legitimate bounds. A judgment speaks most powerfully when it confines itself to the questions sharpened by the adversarial process and resists the allure of prophetic or omniscient pronouncements. By anchoring its voice in the evidence and arguments before it, the court preserves both the coherence of the law and the legitimacy of its authority.

CONCLUDING REFLECTIONS

Judicial writing is not only a vehicle for legal reasoning. It is also the voice of the court. That voice must be marked by respect for those who appear before it and by humility in the exercise of judicial authority.

Together, respect and humility remind us that each judgment is a public act of reasoning that carries institutional weight. A judgment may be doctrinally sound, but if its tone lapses into condescension, spectacle, or emotional indulgence, it risks eroding confidence in the court.

To write with respect and humility is to acknowledge that the court's words do more than decide disputes: they shape how justice is perceived, received, and remembered. In this way, judicial tone is not ornament but substance. It is part of the law's integrity, and part of the court's stewardship of its voice.

To this day, the unwritten line about the unmasking of a masked vigilante stays with me. Not as a missed opportunity for witticism, but as a reminder that a judicious tone is shaped not only by what is written but also by the wisdom to leave certain things unwritten.[50]

NOTES

1 See the discussion in Chapter 4 (on 'Losing the Legal Excess').
2 See the discussion in Chapter 1 (on 'For Whom Do We Write?').
3 As a matter of practice in the Singapore courts, appellate judges do not usually refer to the judge below by name, especially if the decision is being reversed on appeal.
4 A related point was made in the context of 'Overstatement' in Chapter 4.
5 See also the later discussion on 'Sensationalism'.
6 Bo Seo, *Good Arguments: How Debate Teaches Us to Listen and Be Heard* (Penguin Press 2022) 140.
7 [2021] SGHC 187, [2022] 4 SLR 560.
8 *Gaiyathiri* (n 7) 72.
9 *Gaiyathiri* (n 7) 77.
10 Richard Heppner Jr, 'Rooted: Metaphors and Judicial Philosophy in *Artis v District of Columbia*' (2023) 56 Ind L Rev 329, 334.
11 Heppner (n 10) 334, 335.
12 Richard Castle, 'Lord Atkin and the Neighbour Test: Origins of the Principles of Negligence in *Donoghue v Stevenson*' (2003) 33 Eccles L J 210, 213.
13 *Donoghue v Stevenson* [1932] AC 562 (HL) 580.
14 Lord Reed (Speech at the *Donoghue v Stevenson* 90th Anniversary Conference, 'The Immortal Snail', 26 May 2022) <https://perma.cc/M3FC-K27M>.
15 This has been described as a 'spatial metaphor' in Andrew Culley and Michael Salter, 'Why Study Metaphors?' (2004) 15 KLJ 347, 352.
16 *Donoghue* (n 13) 580.
17 Specifically, Jesus' parable of the Good Samaritan in Luke 10:25–37. See Castle (n 12).
18 Culley and Salter (n 15) 352.
19 Heppner (n 10).
20 Elizabeth Thornburg, 'Just Say "No Fishing": The Lure of Metaphor' (2006) 40(1) U Mich J L Ref 1.
21 The use of his phrase has been further considered by the UK Supreme Court in *Healthcare at Home Ltd v Common Services Agency* [2014] UKSC 49.
22 *Edgington v Fitzmaurice* (1885) 29 Ch D 459 (CA) 483 (Bowen LJ).
23 *Gollins v Gollins* [1963] UKHL 5, [1964] AC 644, 664 (Lord Reid).
24 See *Fong Mun v Chan Yuen Lan* [2013] SGHC 99, [2013] 3 SLR 685 [15]. Justice Choo Han Teck credited the metaphor to Lord Mance, who had used it in a different context in *Dallah Real Estate and Tourism Holding Co v Ministry of Religious Affairs of the Government of Pakistan* [2010] UKSC 46, [2011] 1 AC 763 [30].
25 Thomas Ross, 'Metaphor and Paradox' (1989) 23 GLR 1053.
26 Thornburg (n 20) 2.
27 Thornburg (n 20) 3.
28 *Berkey v Third Avenue Railway Co* 244 NY 84, 155 NE 58, 61 (NY 1926).
29 Jack Oakley and Brian Opeskin, 'Banter From the Bench: The Use of Humour in the Exercise of Judicial Functions' (2016) 42 ABR 82, 83.
30 Gerald Lebovits, Alifya Curtin and Lisa Solomon, 'Ethical Judicial Opinion Writing' (2008) 21 Geo J Legal Ethics 237.

31 United States Circuit Judge of the United States Court of Appeals for the Fifth Circuit.

32 Lawrence Vilardo and Howard Gutman, 'In Memoriam: The Honorable Irving L. Goldberg: A Place in History' (1995) 49 SMU L Rev 1, 8.

33 *Kentucky Fried Chicken Corp v Diversified Packaging Corp* 549 F 2d 368 (5th Cir 1977).

34 *Stock v Commissioner* 551 F 2d 614, 615 (5th Cir 1977).

35 In chronological order from the most to the least recent, a limited selection includes:

- Oakley and Opeskin (n 29).
- Sharyn Roach Anleu, Kathy Mack and Jordan Tutton, 'Judicial Humour in the Australian Courtroom' (2014) 38 Melb U L Rev 621.
- Mary Trevor, 'From Ostriches to Sci-Fi: A Social Science Analysis of the Impact of Humor in Judicial Opinions' (2014) 45 U Toledo L Rev 291.
- Jonathan Browning, 'To Boldly Go Where Few Judges Have Gone Before: How the Bench Is Using a Pop-Culture Sci-Fi Classic to Explain Its Decisions' (2013) 76 Tex B J 765.
- Lucas Hori, '*Bons Mots*, Buffoonery, and the Bench: The Role of Humor in Judicial Opinions' (2012) 60 UCLA L Rev Discourse 16.
- Lebovits, Curtin and Solomon (n 30).
- Jay Wexler, 'Laugh Track II – Still Laughin'!' (2007) 117 Yale LJ Pocket Part 130.
- Jay Wexler, 'Laugh Track' (2005) 9 Green Bag 2D 59.
- Sue Trask, 'Humor in Judicial Opinions' in William & Mary Law Library, 'Law Library Briefs, Vol 5, No 4 (January 1994)' (1994) Library Newsletter 29.
- Cameron Harvey, *Legal Wit & Whimsy: An Anthology of Legal Humour* (Carswell 1988) 135–155.
- Adalberto Jordan, 'Imagery, Humor, and the Judicial Opinion' (1987) 41 U Miami L Rev 693.
- William Prosser, *The Judicial Humorist: A Collection of Judicial Opinions and Other Frivolities* (Little Brown 1952)

36 In *Gonzalez-Servin v Ford Motor Co* 662 F 3d 931 (7th Cir 2011), the issue before the court related to *forum non conveniens*. Judge Richard Posner felt that multiple counsel in the case had ignored 'apparently dispositive precedent' when presenting arguments. He verbally compared the tactic to an ostrich burying its head in the sand, but also inserted two photographs into the opinion – one of an ostrich with its head in the sand, and the other of a man wearing a khaki coat (presumably, a lawyer) doing the same.

37 *Productos Carnic SA v Central American Beef and Seafood Trading Co* 621 F 2d 683 (5th Cir 1980). In a lawsuit brought to recover 862,000 pounds of frozen boneless beef from a corporation to which the beef had been shipped, Judge John Brown deployed creatively written headings including 'No Bones About It', 'Appellant's Beef', and 'What's at Steak'.

38 *Fisher v Lowe* 122 Mich App 418, 333 NW 2d 67 (Mich Ct App 1983). In this case, the owner of a tree sued the driver and owner of a car that had crashed into the tree. Judge John Gillis affirmed judgment for the defendants, saying: 'We thought that we would never see / A suit to compensate a tree. / A suit whose claim in tort is prest / Upon a mangled tree's behest; / A tree whose battered trunk was prest / Against a Chevy's crumpled crest; / A tree that faces each new day / With bark and limb in disarray; / A tree that may forever bear / A lasting need for tender care. / Flora lovers though we three, / We must uphold the court's decree.' Another example is found in *Wheat v Fraker* 107 Ga App 318 (1963), where the Court of Appeals of Georgia issued an appellate decision in a 28-line poem (this decision is reproduced in Harvey (n 35) 148–149).

39 In a defamation lawsuit between a neighbour (Mr Bailey) and Eminem (rapper Marshall Mathers), who was upset that Eminem had rapped that Mr Bailey was a bully in middle school, Circuit Court Judge Deborah Servitto found that Eminem's comments were justified. The judge included a 36-line rap in her decision, which include phrases such as 'Bailey also admitted he was a bully in youth / Which makes what Marshall said substantial truth / This doctrine is a defense well known / And renders Bailey's case substantially blown.' See Bill Hoffman, 'Rappin' the Gavel; Judge Busts a Rhyme as She Clears Eminem' *New York Post* (22 October 2003) <https://perma.cc/623Y-T6ZA>.

40 Murray Gleeson AC, 'The Role of the Judge and Becoming a Judge' (Remarks at the National Judicial Orientation Programme, Sydney, 16 August 1998) <https://perma.cc/DTQ6-TCJR>.

41 Jennifer Sheppard, 'The "Write" Way: A Judicial Clerk's Guide to Writing for the Court' (2008) 38 U Balt L Rev 73, 109, 110.

42 *Russell v State* 372 SE 2d 445, 447 (Ga App Ct 1988) (Carley J).

43 *Green v Green* (1989) 17 NSWLR 343 (NSWCA), 346D–E. This case was referenced in Oakley and Opeskin (n 29) 87.

44 Oakley and Opeskin (n 29) 87.

45 Gleeson (n 40).

46 Gleeson (n 40).

47 Gleeson (n 40).

48 Sundaresh Menon, remarks at a closed-door session organised by the Singapore Judicial College on 'Unpacking Judicial Arrogance' (20 July 2017).

49 Andrew Phang, *Towards a New Theory of Adjudication: Integrating Theory and Practice* (Hart Publishing, 2025) 225.

50 As Justice Andrew Phang observed, '[a] clever judge is not necessarily a wise judge': Phang (n 49) 225.

The Writing Room – Judges at Work

Six

'All rise'. The judge departs and the courtroom empties. As lawyers, litigants, journalists, and members of the public file out, low murmurs ripple through the gallery – speculation, relief, disappointment, the quiet unwinding of courtroom tension. The doors shut, and the trial's echoes fade, leaving the case to await its reckoning in the judge's chamber.

And in that chamber, the case lingers – not just in the form of notes or submissions, but as a set of unresolved questions that continue to occupy the judicial mind. Some arguments linger because they were well made; others, because they were not.

This is the threshold – between the collective space of the courtroom, with all its oral posturing and emotion, and the solitary space of the writing room. The judge is now no longer listening, questioning, or responding. Now begins the work of deliberating: of giving shape to reasons, of testing conclusions, of finding the voice in which the court will eventually speak.

The writing room is not always a room in the literal sense. It may be a desk at the end of the day, a quiet moment over lunch, or a walk with a simple voice recorder (more on that later). But it is not only a physical space – it is, as much, a mental one, one shaped by focus, discipline, and the pressures of the judicial role. Indeed, judgment writing often begins in a mind that is crowded with competing priorities, unresolved questions, and uncertainty. This mental congestion can easily give rise to procrastination. Perfectionism may slow the hand as well, because the tendency is to try to write in a judgment-ready fashion from the outset. And beneath these lies the quiet but persistent pressure to 'get it right' from the get-go. These tendencies are familiar features in the writing process, and recognising them is part of preparing oneself for the work ahead.

In this chapter, we step into the metaphorical writing room and trace the typical stages in the journey of crafting a judgment. The process begins with the 'Orientation', where the judge becomes reacquainted with the terrain of the hearing; moves to the challenge

DOI: 10.4324/9781042017027-7

of penning the 'First Words'; considers strategies for sustaining 'Momentum' when a judgment cannot be written in a single sitting; turns to 'Consultation', where conversations with colleagues or assistants can sharpen thinking; and concludes with 'Revision', where the draft is refined for release. These are not rigid steps but recurring practices that help transform the labour of deliberation into a coherent written judgment.

THE ORIENTATION

In the writing room, the work of writing rarely begins with sentences on a page (to crime judges – the pun is purely accidental). It often begins instead with *orientation*: the judge becoming reacquainted with the terrain, through reviewing personal notes, parties' submissions, the evidential record, and the authorities. There is no single method or sequence that suits every case or every judge. Some begin with a mental map of the issues; others plunge into the record first, before sketching the map.

What follows illustrates but one approach that has worked well for me. It is shaped by personal experience and corroborated by the anecdotal practices of some of the judges I have spoken with. Of course, your mileage (as the saying goes) may vary.

The orientation process begins even before the hearing ends. Judges presiding over long or complex hearings may find it helpful to take notes during the proceedings, even if verbatim transcripts of the hearing will be produced. These early notes may record impressions, highlight turning points, or sketch the structure of the eventual judgment. Most of the time they are working reflections, not final views.[1] It can be very helpful to take notes during the hearing or even draft specific extracts of the judgment after standing down from the bench each day. When the time comes to write in earnest, these notes and draft extracts can serve as a map, charting how the issues unfolded in real time and guiding the judge back through the terrain of the hearing. They help anchor the judge's early impressions before they fade, reduce the cognitive load of the orientation process, and therefore serve not only as reminders but also as psychological footholds in coming to grips with the material after the hearing has ended.

Where parties' *submissions* are available, these serve as a useful launch pad. In cases where the party is self-represented or where legal representation is poor, however, the court may not have this luxury. Properly crafted submissions frame the issues, identify the authorities, and offer competing accounts of the case. That said, regardless of the quality of the submissions, the judge should always actively consider whether the issues have been properly identified and whether the framing is complete. After all, the judge is not there simply to accept what is offered by the parties, even if the parties agree. At this stage, I find that my personal in-hearing notes and draft judgment extracts (if any) serve as a vital cross-check, setting the parties' positions against my evolving reflections. I have generally found it useful to prepare a document that sets out the issues raised in the submissions together with the parties' positions on each point, supplemented by my own notes and draft extracts that are marked to clearly distinguish them from the parties' positions (for example, by using different font colours, or by using the 'comment' function in word processing software). Let's call this the 'Orientation Document'.

A review of the *evidential record* follows. This is a time-consuming process. There may be a (strong) temptation to rely on what the parties have stated in their submissions, rather than to dig through a voluminous record. However, the process of independent review is necessary, especially where the judge is playing the role of the factfinder. In this regard, it is rarely possible to absorb the information on record in one sweep. In any event, it is advisable to take the opportunity, when reviewing the evidential record, to begin distinguishing what is relevant from what is not. One way to do so is to annotate and take notes of key pieces of evidence while going through the record. I have found it useful to record the critical points in the Orientation Document, leaving rough-and-ready 'breadcrumbs'. I call them 'breadcrumbs' in the Hansel and Gretel sense: these are markers to help find one's way back through the documentary forest. Such 'breadcrumbs' may take two forms: footnotes that pinpoint specific passages in the record (e.g., 'See Bundle A p 15 para 3') or screenshots from softcopy records that help instantly recall what I meant to capture in my notes. The 'breadcrumbs' seldom appear in the eventual judgment, but they form an invaluable part of the writing process. They are tools that help me return to the source and to remember why a particular path was taken. My future self has always thanked me for the discipline in this exercise; your future self, too, will thank you.

Then come the *authorities*, whether primary or secondary. Whether the authorities cited in the submissions come from Senior Counsel or a self-represented party, the judge's obligation to get the law right remains the same. I generally take notes of each key proposition in the Orientation

Document, writing short statements of how each proposition is relevant to the present case and dropping 'breadcrumbs' to the source authority. The process is almost as if I am building my own *Halsbury's*,[7] customised to the issues at hand. As I read, I also apply my mind to whether the parties' propositions have accurately represented the authorities, whether the authorities remain good law, and whether there may be authorities that have been overlooked. I usually insert notes of my thoughts (as before, using fonts of different colour or the 'comment' function in word processing software).

In recent years, a new form of vigilance has become necessary when reviewing authorities. Shortly after ChatGPT was publicly launched, an American lawyer cited fictitious cases generated by the platform.[3] Since then, the citation of hallucinated cases has featured in courts all around the world.[4] Similar incidents have arisen in Singapore[5] – including one where the judge was himself named as a defendant in a fictitious case.[6] Such episodes underscore why reviewing the authorities in detail is a critical step in the orientation process. The judge must neither rely unthinkingly on what is offered nor be swayed by authorities that misstate the law (or worse, that do not exist at all).

By the time I have completed the aforementioned review (i.e., reviewing personal notes, parties' submissions, the evidential record, and the authorities), the Orientation Document provides a good and detailed overview of all the issues that the judgment must traverse.

THE FIRST WORDS

There is a particular hesitation that comes with setting out the first words of a judgment. This often stems from perfectionism, manifesting in the self-imposed pressure of writing in a judgment-ready fashion from the outset. Having an Orientation Document helps in putting pen to paper, but sometimes even with such a document, there is inertia in penning the first words.

For some judges, the solution is to begin with what feels easiest. This may be the procedural history or a summary of undisputed facts. These sections may not be the most intellectually demanding, but precisely because of that, they offer a quick way to make progress. They allow the writing to begin without the pressure of resolving the most difficult issues first. Beginning with what feels manageable can help blunt the force of procrastination and perfectionism, and also prod one along in the process of gaining precious momentum. Of course, not everyone operates in the same way. Some judges prefer to start with the core reasoning and to tackle the crucial legal arguments first, even if it means writing in fragments. There is no single right approach. What matters is finding a point of entry that allows the judgment to start taking shape.

One method that some judges find helpful is what might be called a 'brain dump': writing down thoughts, opinions, impressions, and tentative conclusions without worrying about structure or polish. Professor Betty Flowers referred to this as the 'madman' stage of writing, where a person 'writes crazily and perhaps rather sloppily'.[7] The goal of the 'brain dump' is not to produce a usable draft judgment but to externalise thinking by putting forward one's thoughts so that one has a starting point. It is aimed at helping to lower the psychological barrier to commencing the writing process. If the Orientation Document is logically and comprehensively put together, it may well provide a useable framework for the 'brain dump'.

The 'brain dump' can be done in writing. But it can also be done by speaking aloud. For those who find dictation a powerful tool, voice can be a way into thought. In my own practice, I sometimes find that speaking aloud, even if just to myself or into a voice recorder, frees my mind from the constraints of writing or typing and allows my thoughts to emerge more rapidly. In certain settings, being on my feet can force a kind of focus that staring at a blank page (or blank screen) does not. What begins as a rough oral articulation can first be captured in a voice recorder, then played back or transcribed to help shape the structure of the judgment and ease the task of putting pen to paper.

I once thought that this soliloquy approach to judgment writing was an esoteric habit and thus hesitated to suggest it to others. Yet that hesitation lessened when I encountered an unexpected source of validation in an episode of *Elementary*, the CBS television series offering a modern take on Sherlock Holmes. In one scene, Holmes tells his associate, Dr Joan (not John) Watson:[8]

> *I've found, over the years, that nothing clears up a difficult case so much as stating it to another person. I talk, they listen, and in talking, I make connections I may have otherwise missed. One-way street, not two.*

Holmes added that one need not speak aloud to some*one*; it may suffice to speak to some*thing*:[9]

> *For a brief stretch in London, I talked only to a phrenology bust I kept in my study. I named him Angus.*

As eccentric as it may sound, Holmes' method aligns with elements of dialogic learning and the Socratic method, albeit with a twist. His 'one-way street' is not a dialogue in the traditional sense, but a form of clarifying his own thoughts. Speaking aloud helped him to gather his thoughts, expose gaps, and sharpen reasoning. It enabled reflection on reasoning, mimicking the iterative development of ideas that characterises dialogic learning. It forced a kind of organisation and clarity akin to responding to Socratic questioning.

Whether you begin with what feels easiest or with a brain dump of anything and everything that comes to mind, it is crucial to remember that the first words of a judgment do not need to be perfect. They need only to begin the work. At this stage, consciously set aside the 'critical energy' that drives you to evaluate and refine your writing.[10] That discipline comes later; for now, the task is simply to get words moving.

THE MOMENTUM

Writing can build momentum. There are moments when you feel in full flight – when the reasoning is clear, the structure is coherent, and the words arrive in step with thought. But momentum is fragile. It can be lost to external interruptions, fatigue, the complexity of the issue at hand, or even the urge to endlessly polish earlier sections.

Few judgments are written in a single sitting. Most are written in fragments, across days or weeks, between hearings, meetings, and other demands. The temptation to delay returning to the draft can grow, especially when the next section feels difficult. Here, I suggest three techniques to help maintain momentum in judgment writing: the Hemingway Bridge, the Pomodoro Technique, and spatial strategies.

Hemingway Bridge

One technique that I have taught at judgment writing programmes, and which I used extensively in writing this book, is what may be referred to as the 'Hemingway Bridge'. This naming is in honour of a method Ernest Hemingway described in a 1958 interview about his process of fictional writing. In that interview, he explained that when writing a book or a story:[11]

> *You write until you come to a place where you still have your juice and know what will happen next and you stop and try to live through until the next day when you hit it again.*

This technique was originally expressed as a tool for creative writing. But as it is really a tool for maintaining a writer's momentum, it also works well in other forms of writing such as judgment writing (which one hopes is anything but fictional). Indeed, the Hemingway Bridge method of maintaining a state of 'flow' has even been deployed in contexts as varied as the building of guitars.[12] The idea is simple: one should stop writing while one still knows what comes next. That way, the return to the task will be easier the next day, because one has already built a *bridge* from the end of the first work period to the start of the second.

In practice, this means resisting the urge to write to the very last minute. If time is running short, it can be more helpful to dedicate the final 15 or 20 minutes to sketching out what remains: questions to resolve, points to clarify, or even a rough sentence to begin the next section. It is a small act of continuity, but it can make the difference between resuming and restarting. It can help judgment writers, like fiction authors, maintain their momentum despite the inevitable disruptions of life.

Pomodoro Technique

Another useful technique, particularly for managing time and sustaining focus during writing, is the Pomodoro Technique. The Pomodoro Technique was developed by Francesco Cirillo in the late 1980s. As a university student, he used a tomato-shaped kitchen timer ('pomodoro' is Italian for tomato) to break his study sessions into short, focused intervals. Each interval – typically 25 minutes – is known as a 'pomodoro' and is followed by a short break.

In judgment writing, such intervals can serve as manageable, low-pressure goals that honour both concentration and rest. Instead of approaching the task with vague ambition or perfectionistic anxiety, one can set specific, time-bound goals, such as 'write for 25 minutes, uninterrupted, and stop there', 'complete the background section in two hours', and 'analyse one legal issue before lunch'.

These goals are modest in scope, but clear in direction. The short breaks between the intervals are part of the rhythm, helping the mind to reset and return to the task at hand.

Spatial Strategies

A third way to sustain momentum is to attend to the space in which one writes. Space can be harnessed in two complementary ways: by *preserving* it to ensure continuity, or by *resetting* it to stimulate fresh thinking. I have found both methods useful. Indeed, I often use a combination of both in the course of writing a single judgment, depending on the nature of the judgment and the stage of the drafting.

Preserving the environment means deliberately leaving the workspace arranged so that the next day begins with continuity rather than inertia. Where one has the privilege of a secure space to leave materials untouched, spatial memory can be enlisted. Reference works, evidential records, authorities, and submissions may be left open at the very page where work paused. Returning to these physical cues often allows the writer to pick up the thread immediately, without retracing steps or relocating sources. The same principle applies in the digital workspace. I sometimes leave a bookmark in the (PDF[13]) documents I am perusing, or insert a note to self in the draft judgment (such as '[*Pick up here*]'), so that I can quickly locate the point where I left off. These markers, whether physical or digital, preserve continuity and reduce the friction of resuming the task.

Resetting the environment works in the opposite way. It does not so much create momentum as restore it. When monotony or fatigue break the flow, even small adjustments – rearranging the desk, altering the lighting, turning on soothing music tracks, or introducing plants – can refresh the mind and sharpen focus. At times, a more dramatic change of setting may be helpful. Writing in a library, a café, or even outdoors can alter one's perspective and provide new energy. I have also found it useful to write in settings buffered from the daily grind, where interruptions are fewer and focus can deepen. For instance, significant segments of this book were written while on flights between Singapore and Beijing, New York, Tokyo, and Sydney, as well as on rail services such as America's Acela Express and Amtrak, and Japan's *Shinkansen* and Romancecar. These wonderful journeys, though filled with no shortage of welcome distractions, offered stretches of time in new environments that proved highly conducive to my writing. When momentum falters, a change of place or atmosphere can act as a catalyst, helping the writer to re-enter the flow of thought.

Together, these spatial strategies remind us that writing is not only a mental act but also a physical one, shaped by the surroundings in which it occurs. Harnessing the space around us can help sustain or restore the momentum of judgment writing.

THE CONSULTATION

Consultation and conversation with others can help sharpen the clarity of one's thoughts. Such discussions are most effective once the judge has already prepared a draft, for it is the judge's own reasoning that must be tested. I discuss this from the perspectives of *purpose*, *principle*, and *practice*, in the context of a single-judge court. Different considerations apply in multi-judge panels.

Purpose

The purpose of consultation is not to outsource judgment, but to sharpen it.

Judging is each individual judge's responsibility. Singapore's Judicial Code of Conduct affirms – as do many other judicial codes – that judges must 'demonstrate independence in their individual decision-making' and are 'solely responsible for their respective decisions'.[14]

But judicial independence does not require judicial isolation. Many judges find it helpful to discuss their reasoning with others who can provide useful feedback – colleagues, law clerks, or judicial assistants. Consultation, when approached judiciously, can be a vital part of the thinking process. It allows the articulation of the judge's own reasoning to a counterpart, thus surfacing tensions, testing assumptions, encountering alternative perspectives, and refining the expression of difficult points. It can also temper the perfectionistic instinct to refine a draft endlessly, for even a brief exchange with a colleague can reveal weaknesses or affirm strengths in what one has already written.

Principle

All consultation must be guided by the principle of ownership. The judge must remain the owner of the reasoning, not merely the endorser or passive recipient of another's thinking.

A helpful question to ask is: 'Am I testing my thoughts or delegating the thought process?' The former is part of the craft, while the latter is a failure of it. At its best, consultation strengthens not only the individual judgment but also the collegial culture of the judiciary. It fosters shared learning, mentorship, and resilience. In this way, consultation becomes more than a tool for individual clarity; it helps enhance judging as a craft.

Practice

As a matter of practice, consultation can take many forms. It may be formal or informal, oral or written. A law clerk's or judicial assistant's memorandum, a colleague's probing question, or even a casual exchange over coffee can each sharpen reasoning in different ways. Judges may consult to clarify ambiguities, stress-test arguments, or expose blind spots that solitary reflection might miss.

Yet consultation has boundaries. Where the discussion relates to a specific case rather than a general legal issue of academic interest, the judge should not seek input from judges higher in the hierarchy (especially since an appeal may lie to them or their counterparts) or from others outside the judiciary.

Consultation also inevitably invites another person's opinion. That is not a weakness, provided the judge has already formed a preliminary view. Entering the discussion with one's own reasoning ensures that feedback is received as a test of thought rather than as a substitute for it. The judge should therefore lead the consultation by putting forward the judge's own reasoning and inviting critique, rather than waiting for another to suggest solutions. Even where the judge wishes to avoid 'priming' the counterpart, this is no excuse for failing to form an undisclosed personal and preliminary view.

THE REVISION

There is a well-worn adage among writers: there is no good writing, only good rewriting. The same holds true for written judgments. Rarely does a first draft say exactly what it needs to say, in precisely the way it needs to be said. Revising and editing a judgment is a mark of care and responsibility for this important task. This stage is where perfectionist tendencies and the pressure to 'get it right' find their rightful place, for here they sharpen rather than stall the work.

Some judges edit in waves, for instance, targeting structure first, then tone, then citations. This layered approach allows each concern to be addressed in turn, rather than juggled all at once. Professor Edward Berry suggests a seven-stage checklist for revision.[15] It can serve as a useful starting point, although many judges develop their own routines over time.

Reading the draft aloud can be surprisingly effective. Awkward phrasing, missing words, or unintended sharpness often reveal themselves more clearly to the ear than to the eye. Accessibility tools such as the 'Read Aloud' function in Microsoft Word can serve this purpose well. What the eyes gloss over, the ears may catch.

Time away from the draft can also help. Some distance allows the mind to reset, and what once seemed settled may now appear in need of refinement. Jennifer Sheppard recommends setting the draft aside before editing, noting that a fresh view can reveal both larger issues (such as faulty reasoning or poor organisation) and smaller ones (like missing citations or repeated words).[16]

Taking pause before revisiting the draft can help spare one the embarrassment of overlooked typographical errors. These are easy to miss when the eye is too familiar with the text. They can be more (or even glaringly) obvious to a reader coming to the judgment afresh. After all, malapropisms[17] are not confined to boxing legends. Mike Tyson's 'fade into Bolivian' (oblivion)[18] has its judicial counterparts, such as a confident declaration that an issue was 'mute' (moot), that the 'statue' (statute) of limitations bars a claim, or that the parties should pursue 'meditation' (mediation).[19]

Errors in blockquotes are also especially easy to miss, since we tend to skip over them – just as our readers do.[20] I once discovered (thankfully!) that I had accidentally typed my password into a blockquote. Because blockquotes tend to fade into the background of a draft, I nearly overlooked it. Fortunately, I caught the mistake before publication and was able to remove it. As unnoticed slips can easily creep into block quotes, it is critical to check them with special care.

Where possible, having a trusted other cast a second pair of eyes over the judgment can be invaluable. A colleague or clerk may notice what you have missed, catch typographical slips, terminological inconsistencies, or lapses in citation, or even highlight points where the reasoning is abrupt, the transitions unclear, or assumptions left unstated. Because the writer is often too close to the text, blind spots are inevitable; a fresh reader sees the judgment as the eventual audience will.

CONCLUDING REFLECTIONS

Writing a judgment is rarely a smooth experience. Often, the process stalls, doubles back, and involves considerable labour if not frustration. Yet this very struggle is part of the craft.

The techniques described in this chapter – orientation, first words, momentum, consultation, and revision – are not formulaic tricks but ways of navigating the metaphorical writing room. They help the judge move from the outward contest of voices to the inward discipline of reasoning, and finally to the articulation of a single coherent response. They help steady the mind against the familiar pressures that accompany the task: the hesitation of beginning, the pull of perfectionism, and the responsibility to 'get it right'. However painful the journey, each draft and each revision contributes to a stronger written judgment.

This chapter began with the image of the courtroom doors closing. It ends with the reminder that those doors eventually open again, when the judgment is delivered. At this time, the judge's labour in the writing room becomes a public act of explanation, where the painstaking writing process is transformed into the authoritative voice of reason.

NOTES

1 Although they may be final determinations in some situations, such as decisions on standalone or preliminary issues or on trials within trials (such as the *voir dire* of crime trials).

2 Widely relied upon across the Commonwealth common law world, *Halsbury's Laws* are comprehensive multi-volume legal encyclopaedias. They provide an authoritative narrative statement of the law, systematically arranged by subject, with detailed classification of issues and extensive cross-references to statutes, cases, and secondary authorities.

3 *Mata v Avianca, Inc* 678 F Supp 3rd 443 (SDNY 2023).

4 For instance, in Canada, a lawyer had relied on AI to draft submissions, which included citations to cases that did not exist. The lawyer later explained that he had misunderstood the tool, thinking that it was a search engine that would return reliable and citeable results. She was ultimately ordered to pay the other party's costs, having sent them on a fruitless search for non-existent cases. See Leyland Cecco, 'Canada Lawyer Under Fire for Submitting Fake Cases Created by AI Chatbot' *The Guardian* (29 February 2024) <https://perma.cc/Z3WH-2H8K>; Jason Proctor, 'BC Lawyer Reprimanded for Citing Fake Cases Invented by ChatGPT' *CBC News* (26 February 2024) <https://perma.cc/H9C7-6HV2>.

5 See, for instance, *Tan Hai Peng Micheal and another v Tan Cheong Joo and another* [2026] SGHC 49 and *Tajudin bin Gulam Rasul v Suriaya bte Haja Mohideen* [2025] SGHCR 33.

6 Natalie Skead and Justin Yeo, 'Judicial Education in a Brave New World' (2025) 59 Law Teach 666, fn 23. This is also mentioned in Chapter 8, text accompanying n 51.

7 Betty Flowers, 'Madman, Architect, Carpenter, Judge: Roles and the Writing Process' (1981) 58 Language Arts 834.

8 *Elementary*, Season 1, Episode 3 (CBS, 2012).

9 *Elementary*, Season 1, Episode 3 (CBS, 2012).

10 Flowers (n 7) 834.

11 This is drawn from an interview of Ernest Hemingway by George Plimpton: The Paris Review, 'Ernest Hemingway, The Art of Fiction No 21' (Spring 1958) <https://www.theparisreview.org/interviews/4825/the-art-of-fiction-no-21-ernest-hemingway> accessed 23 April 2026.

12 Tom Bills, 'The Hemingway Bridge Method & How To Use It' (*The Art of Lutherie*) <https://perma.cc/4DPS-AVMY>.

13 Portable Document Format, a file format developed by Adobe Inc in 1993.

14 Singapore Courts, 'Singapore Judicial Code of Conduct for the Judges and Judicial Commissioners of the Supreme Court of Singapore' (11 October 2024) <https://perma.cc/X5LK-EG2C> 5.

15 Edward Berry, *Writing Reasons: A Handbook for Judges* (6th edn, LexisNexis Canada 2025) 139–141.

16 Jennifer Sheppard, 'The "Write" Way: A Judicial Clerk's Guide to Writing for the Court' (2008) 38 U Balt L Rev 73, 110, 111.

17 The expression 'malapropism' traces back to Mrs Malaprop in Richard Brinsley Sheridan's 1775 play, *The Rivals*. Her name comes from the French '*mal à propos*', meaning 'inappropriate', and she became famous for consistently substituting incorrect, though similar-sounding, words for the ones she intended.

18 Bill Simmons, 'Say "goodbye" to our little friend' (ESPN) <https://perma.cc/US7U-KWGE>.

19 There is a view that the 'mute' (moot) error is an 'eggcorn' (acorn), which is a form of malapropism that happens to make sense. See e.g. Scolaro Law, 'Your Lawyer Is Not Immune to Statue of Limitations, Eggcorns and Malapropisms' (11 June 2024) <https://perma.cc/5VT7-BDXC>.

20 See the discussion in Chapter 2 (on 'Digesting, Not Dumping').

From Bench to Browser – Judgment Writing for a Digital World

Seven

I spent most of my legal education reading judgments on paper – highlighted, annotated, and dog-eared over time. I recall the endless days of photocopying decisions from published law reports. And even when decisions were available online, I gravitated toward printouts. The tactile engagement somehow felt essential to understanding.

When I joined the Singapore judiciary, the first-generation electronic filing system (known as 'EFS') was in operation and documents were increasingly filed online. With the subsequent transition to a second-generation electronic filing system known as eLitigation, the momentum gathered for a move towards a paperless (or, more accurately, 'paper-less') court. Yet electronically filed documents were still routinely printed and bound for the court's reading convenience. Judgments, too, were largely consumed in that same hardcopy fashion.

But in recent years, the reliance on hardcopies has slowly but surely faded. Today, the journey of written reasons – from bench to browser – is increasingly dominated by electronic platforms. Readers today inhabit a different world. A world defined by search bars, hyperlinks, rapid scrolling, tab switching, and AI-generated 'TL; DR' ('Too Long; Didn't Read') summaries. Our reading habits have been reshaped by broader cultural and technological shifts. The proliferation of web-based reading, e-books, and softcopy documents means that text is everywhere – easily accessible at all times, yet paradoxically more transient than ever.

Judgments are now no longer solely perused with highlighter or pen in hand, with attention stretched across margins and pages. An increasing proportion of the legal community and the general public access and digest judgments on screens. I personally know of excellent lawyers who not only can, but regularly do, conduct comprehensive legal research entirely on six-inch mobile phone displays. Judgments are pulled from databases, shared in messaging apps or email correspondence, consumed in flicks and swipes, and sometimes reported (or misreported) in 280 characters[1] or less.

DOI: 10.4324/9781042017027-8

This shift is not only in technology or in the medium of consumption. It is also cognitive. Online readers increasingly read diagonally,[2] in 'F-shaped' patterns (i.e., reading across the top few lines, but gradually fewer of each subsequent line as they read down the webpage) if the block of text has no visual signposts;[3] or in 'layer cake' patterns (i.e., glancing at each heading and skipping over the section if considered irrelevant) if the text is laid out in clear sections with headings.[4] These habits are not signs of laziness but rather of adaptation. Web readers have learnt that scanning is often more efficient than reading and affords them more time to consult multiple sources.[5]

Digital reading influences how readers engage with text, often with the result of decreased attention[6] and discontinuous or even fragmented reading.[7] In hypertext environments, common to most online media, this is compounded by a 'psychological urge to click; an uneasy wariness of mind and index finger'.[8]

Yet even as courts embraced electronic filing and spoke of going 'paperless', judgments have often continued to be delivered as if destined primarily for paper. It remains a curious paradox: in a digital environment, readers are still handed PDFs formatted for printing, complete with fixed pagination and margins. This practice not only strongly encourages printing for ease of use but also assumes a mode of consumption that no longer reflects how judgments are actually read – increasingly on screens, in databases, or on mobile devices. The challenge, then, is to ask how our judgments can be maximally accessible in the medium of consumption, rather than merely replicating the conventions of print.

The act of judgment writing now arguably carries new burdens relating to designing for digital readability and digital comprehension. The rest of this chapter reflects on the identified burdens, how we may be able to attend to them and, in so doing, meet our readers not where they were but where they are. Some of these points may apply more directly to judicial administrators and systems reformers than judges. Judges should nonetheless take note[9] for they are often in positions of authority to shape how the court's reasoning travels from bench to browser, echoes through cyberspace, and endures in the collective memory of the internet-powered public domain.

DESIGNING FOR DIGITAL READABILITY

Judgments were once written for readers who set aside time to read them linearly, page by page. Today, the reader arrives differently – descending rapidly, on a screen, and possibly even mid-hearing while searching for a quick answer to a pressing issue. They scroll, skim, and search. In this digital landscape, how a judgment is presented may affect whether it is read and understood at all.

As alluded to earlier, numerous studies have examined how readers consume information on screens. One of the key reports details a comprehensive study involving eye-tracking analysis of more than 300 people, using hundreds of websites,[10] resulting in a report exceeding 300 pages, containing 83 design recommendations. The second edition of the report exceeded 400 pages, involved over 500 participants, and included 62 recommendations.[11]

Not all the recommendations, however, apply to judgments. Judicial writing is not commercial content: we are not primarily interested in motivating uninterested readers to read more or in garnering clicks. Still, these reports provide gems of wisdom for the practice of judgment writing. They help us to understand that each individual user's level of motivation has a significant effect on the time a reader is willing to spend, which in turn shapes reading behaviour.[12] In the context of judgments, we can assume that readers are 'motivated' readers – they persist in reading not because they enjoy the exercise (although some do), but because they have a personal stake or interest in it, whether as parties, researchers, or commentators. However, even motivated readers bring with them some familiar digital habits of scanning, searching, and selective attention. Judgment readability must therefore take account of these habits.

At the institutional level, many courts already employ judgment templates featuring stylesheets designed to ensure a consistent and professional visual presentation, or front matter that provides the administrative detail to identify each case. Such conventions serve a vital institutional purpose: they reinforce the identity of the court and help readers navigate judgments with a shared set of expectations. A consistent structure and format across judgments not only helps to make reader comprehension more efficient but also fosters trust in the judicial process as it signals that each decision is part of a coherent and principled tradition. Against this backdrop, nothing I say here should be construed as encouraging judges to format their judgments as they please in the name of aiding digital comprehension. Judicial writing must remain institutionally anchored, adhering to the judiciary's established house-style and formal requirements. Rather, the thoughts I advance are points for consideration if there is impetus – whether from judicial administrators, reform committees, or design teams – to revisit how a judiciary's judgments are presented in a digital world.

Typography and Layout

Traditional judgment formatting – typically serif fonts, full justification, minimal typographic variations, dense walls of text, and alphabetic margin markers – was designed for print. It exuded formality, elegance, and professionalism. However, on screens, these same features can become barriers. Certain design choices may help to ease the cognitive burden of screen-based reading. Here, I suggest six considerations to keep in mind.

First, the font face used. Serif fonts (such as Times New Roman or Garamond, marked by ornamental stroke endings) are elegant in print. Serif typefaces were traditionally thought to aid reading because the added stroke endings were believed to help distinguish letters, accentuate the main vertical strokes, and provide horizontal cues that assisted the eye in tracking a line of text.[13] In the digital environment, however, the position was reversed: serif typefaces were often considered less readable on screen than their sans-serif counterparts (such as Arial or Helvetica), which lack stroke endings.[14] This is because sans-serif fonts tend to render more cleanly on digital displays, especially smaller screens, due to their simpler letterforms and reduced visual noise. That said, with the proliferation of high-resolution displays, research on typographical legibility is increasingly inconclusive as to which kind of typeface is more legible on screen.[15] Ultimately, much depends on the specific serif or sans-serif font in question.[16]

Second, full justification of text can create uneven spacing between and within words, disrupting visual rhythm. Large blocks of text have always been difficult to read on paper – and this challenge is multiplied on screen. In the context of digital text, left justification can be easier to read as it provides a consistent left margin[17] while avoiding the aforementioned uneven spacing. An option for the reader to display the text in multiple columns[18] rather than single wide column can be useful for landscape-style wide-screen devices (as most computer screens are), especially given the general typographic guideline that an optimal line length for comfortable reading is about 10–15 English words.

Third, differentiating typography for headings, quotations, or emphasis adds navigational clarity. These are not merely decorative. They signal hierarchy, guide attention, and help the reader locate themselves within the judgment's structure. For instance, headings should stand out, as they serve their role only if they 'actually look like headings'.[19] They should be easily distinguishable from the surrounding text (for instance, they should be larger, bolder, or with more whitespace), although they should not be so different as to be an eyesore or distract the reader.[20] Similarly, having a different font face or indentation for quotations can help readers recognise that they are reading quoted text, rather than the main text of the judgment itself.

Fourth, shorter paragraphs are easier to digest on screens, where dense blocks of text can appear overwhelming. Sufficient line spacing – ideally 1.15 to 1.5 lines – allows the eye to move comfortably from one line to the next, reducing fatigue and improving retention. Whitespace (both between sections and paragraphs and in relation to page margins) also plays a vital role in pacing. It invites pause, marks transitions, and gives the judgment room to 'breathe', especially when navigating complex reasoning.

Fifth, paragraph numbering is useful – if not essential – for facilitating pin-point cross-referencing. It is particularly critical if adaptive formatting (discussed later) is adopted. Page numbers (sometimes supported with alphabetic margin markers), once a staple of printed judgments, offer a parallel system of reference, but because they depend on fixed pagination and static layouts, they are less suited to digital environments where text reflows across devices.

Sixth, incorporating smart structural elements into the document ensures that its architecture serves functional accessibility. When headings are properly coded in electronic versions of a judgment (rather than simply styled visually), they become machine readable. This aids readers who rely on navigation tools,[21] screen readers, or other accessibility technologies. It also allows judgments to be searched, indexed, and navigated more efficiently, ensuring that digital presentation supports both human comprehension and technological accessibility.

Towards Adaptive Formatting

It is no longer sufficient to transplant print-based formatting wholesale onto digital platforms. The onscreen environment presents distinct cognitive and ergonomic challenges that require tailored solutions.

A judgment designed solely for print, when rendered on a phone or tablet computer, can become visually dense, difficult to navigate, and cognitively taxing. Instead, the onscreen format should leverage tools that support digital reading: adjustable font sizes to accommodate different devices and visual needs,[22] responsive layouts that adapt to screen dimensions, and possibly a 'reading mode' that minimises distractions by stripping away peripheral interface elements. These features allow the reader to engage with the judgment on their own terms, in their own context, without compromising the integrity of the reasoning.

To be clear, this is not a call to abandon the best practices of print-based judgment writing. The elegance, structure, and typographic discipline of traditional formatting continue to be salutary for printed publications. However, with the use of liquid text,[23] stylesheets[24] and other formatting technologies, the same textual content can be rendered differently across platforms without compromising its integrity. Judgments can thus retain their traditional appearance in print while adopting more readable conventions online. In this model, certain features become critical to preserving continuity: for instance, paragraph numbering and tagging provides stable anchors for cross-referencing and citations, ensuring that references remain consistent across platforms, whether in print or digital form. Another possibility is to consider e-book conventions such as Kindle-style location numbering, which can pinpoint with even greater specificity than paragraph numbers (each 'location' corresponds to about 25 words), although these may not work well in printed versions.

Together with responsive layouts and adjustable fonts, paragraph or location numbering allows judgments to travel faithfully between media. Each medium invites its own mode of engagement, and thoughtful formatting ensures that the reader, whether holding a bound volume or scrolling on a screen, encounters a judgment optimised for the situation at hand.

Above the Fold

In the judgment formats adopted by many jurisdictions, the standard front matter often contains detailed administrative information (such as parties' names, case numbers, related cases or appeals, and so on) about the decision rather than the decision itself.

The average online reader spends an average of 96 seconds on a blog post, and reading time falls below 10 seconds if the post takes 14 minutes or more to finish.[25] While judicial decisions are not blog posts, it remains instructive to consider how digital attention spans shape engagement with text. In a digital world, there is a relatively short cognitive window within which a judgment must signal its relevance and readability. An eye-tracking study demonstrated that users spend about 57% of their page-viewing time 'above the fold' (i.e., the part that appears on screen upon accessing the judgment) and 74% of viewing time above the first two screenfuls.[26] Below the fold, there is a sharp decrease in attention.[27]

As such, the part 'above the fold' takes on added significance for judgments that are consumed online. A cluttered or visually dense opening can deter engagement, while a clean, well-structured beginning invites it. While the standard front matter is important, it is often not essential initial reading for a judgment reader. It may be worthwhile considering compressing the administrative front matter of judgments as much as possible to maximise reader engagement above the fold.

WRITING FOR DIGITAL COMPREHENSION

Judgments must not only be legally sound; they must also be comprehensible to those who read them. In the digital age, comprehension takes on new dimensions. Readers often encounter judgments on screens, where attention is fragmented. A holding buried midway through a 60-page decision may be correct in law but practically invisible. Meanwhile, a comment on a tangential issue may inadvertently attract disproportionate attention if it is vividly phrased or structurally prominent.

Techniques to Facilitate Digital Comprehension

There are ways to optimise judgments to facilitate digital comprehension. The good news is that most of these techniques are consistent with best practices in judgment writing generally (that we have already explored in previous chapters), although they do gain added significance in the digital world. I highlight just three points of special relevance to digital comprehension.

First, it is even more important to write concisely,[28] because complex sentences and long paragraphs – already challenging in print – become yet more difficult to digest on screen.[29]

Second, using appropriate headings[30] can help a digital reader understand the judgment better. The eye-tracking study mentioned earlier revealed that appropriately designed headings make it much easier for users to read content on webpages – they are 'the single most important thing'[31] that one can do to help users consume digital content, especially when the headings 'visually pop as compared to body text'.[32] How the headings are written is equally critical: they should be concise and informative for digital readers.[33]

Third, placing key conclusions at the start of a section and adopting a point-first approach[34] takes on greater importance in the digital world.

As mentioned in the introduction to this chapter, studies on digital readability show that online readers often read diagonally, or in 'F-shaped' or 'layer-cake' patterns.[35] A short, clearly framed paragraph that sets out key conclusions or points caters to these reading habits and also ensures that the judgment's content is accessible to those who must quickly assess its relevance. While the common law's long-form tradition remains essential for explaining nuance, it will be very helpful for digital readers if the key conclusions or points are visible and navigable, rather than buried deep within dense prose.

Fourth, using framing phrases to signal the importance of key points can enhance searchability by search engines and improve how judgments are understood by readers and increasingly ubiquitous artificial intelligence ('AI') tools. Expressions such as 'The central issue in this case is . . .' or 'This conclusion is critical to the outcome' can help alert readers and technology platforms alike to moments of significance. Conversely, when offering incidental or ancillary observations (*obiter dicta*), it is important to signal their limited weight, such as 'This issue does not arise for determination, but may warrant future consideration'. These contextual cues can help prevent peripheral commentary from being mistaken for the court's holding. Indeed, the ability to distinguish the holding (*ratio decidendi*) from such *obiter dicta* is critical for legal AI systems. This task has been described as 'particularly difficult . . . as the original court does not explicitly label them'.[36]

A further point bears mention. Judgments increasingly sit alongside complementary communication modalities such as media summaries and explanatory notes. These ancillary materials serve different purposes and audiences – frequently, the broader public rather than the parties or the profession – and therefore permit a more targeted use of lay language or narrative framing. These complementary modalities further enable courts to calibrate communication across channels and for different audiences, ensuring that the judgment remains doctrinally rigorous while other formats convey its essence in ways suited to specific platforms and readerships.

Can We Rely on AI to Assist Reader Comprehension?

With increasingly powerful AI platforms, one might ask whether we still need to concern ourselves so deeply with digital readability or comprehensibility. Here, the focus is on AI tools that assist *readers*, such as platforms that summarise, signpost, or extract key points from judgments. Can we not simply say, 'Let judges write in whatever way they like. Let the AI platforms, especially purpose-built legal summarisation tools, manage the tasks of summarising, signposting, and searching'? After all, algorithms can already extract holdings, identify keywords, and summarise judgments in seconds.[37] Advancements in technology may also allow users to ask questions about the document at hand.[38] This view suggests that judges need only be concerned about legal reasoning (which is what judges arguably do best), while issues of readability and comprehensibility can be outsourced to computing power (which AI is increasingly well placed to do). The view has intuitive appeal, but I urge caution in completely outsourcing comprehension to AI summary tools, for two reasons: concerns about the accuracy of AI summaries and concerns about AI's ability to communicate tone.

First, concerns about the *accuracy of AI summaries*. Language inherently contains immense complexity, and even two native English speakers may struggle to understand each other if they arrive at the conversation in different contexts. A memorable example is that given by leading AI entrepreneur Nigel Toon. Toon described how he was riding in a London cab in 2021, when the driver said:[39]

> *Did you hear about Ronaldo? They'll play much better now, don't you think? I heard that it was the governor that made it happen. City must be really upset.*

As a long-time purveyor of English football, I instantly knew what the driver was referring to. But this was because I already had the necessary context to the driver's comment, shaped by my awareness of what had gone on in the red half of Manchester in 2021 (again, a reference that not every English speaker may appreciate – the 'red half of Manchester' refers to the English Premier League football club Manchester United). For those of us less steeped in the exploits of the 'Red Devils' (not a cross between a Tasmanian Devil and a Red Panda, but a nickname for Manchester United in this context – indeed, a similar nickname applies to the Belgian national football team, which could confuse even native English speakers with an appreciation of football), the driver's remark would need much more unpacking. As Toon explains, one first needs to decipher that the context of the comment relates to 'football' (or, to American English speakers, 'soccer'); that 'Ronaldo' refers to the Portuguese superstar footballer Cristiano Ronaldo (and not that also-phenomenal and legendary Brazilian footballer Ronaldo Nazario) who had just rejoined Manchester United from Italian football club Juventus; that 'they' therefore refers to Manchester United, that the 'governor' refers not to a politician or public authority but to the highly successful former football manager (or, in the American context, 'coach') Sir Alex Ferguson who had previously brought Ronaldo to Manchester United when he (i.e., Ferguson) was still helming the Red Devils; and that 'City' refers specifically to Manchester United's cross-town rival Manchester City (the 'blue half of Manchester'), which was rumoured to have also tried to sign Ronaldo.

I fed the London cab driver's statement into two different large language models ('LLMs') and asked that each LLM explain the statement to an uninitiated person, making clear what is going on and who is involved. The first LLM returned this explanation:

> *Cristiano Ronaldo plays for a Saudi club called Al Nassr. Recently, something happened that's expected to make the team much stronger – maybe a new signing, a financial boost, or a problem being solved. People are saying it wasn't just normal club business but that a powerful regional governor stepped in to make it happen. Fans of rival teams, like Manchester City, are jokingly said to be annoyed because it gives Ronaldo's team an extra advantage.*

The second LLM offered a less polished but more accurate (albeit still inaccurate and incomplete) explanation:

> *One of the greatest players in the world had to choose a team. A rival club (Manchester City) almost signed him. At the last moment, he joined his old club (Manchester United) instead. Fans think United will improve because of him. City supporters are disappointed they missed out. Talk about a "governor" is probably misunderstanding or gossip about influential people persuading him.*

I give this example because it vividly illustrates how much meaning in natural language depends on shared context, background knowledge, and culturally embedded inference. The cab driver's remark is easy for a football-literate listener to decode, yet opaque to anyone lacking the relevant domain knowledge. AI systems face the same challenge: without the right contextual scaffolding, they may produce explanations that are fluent but flawed.

This is not merely a curiosity of football gossip; it mirrors the risks in legal interpretation. In the context of judgments, a holding buried deep in conditional phrasing, a ratio surrounded by caveats, or a test articulated without clarity may all be overlooked or misunderstood by LLMs. Even relatively simple linguistic devices such as double negatives may be misinterpreted by LLMs. Oblique expressions (such as 'this outcome may seem at odds with earlier decisions, but can be reconciled on closer analysis' or 'it is unnecessary to decide the point conclusively, but the following observations may assist in future cases') may not accurately survive an AI summary. While AI models are increasingly sophisticated, they remain fallible, as seen in routine disclaimers to that effect. They continue to struggle to infer nuance, emphasis, or intent, especially when they lack the necessary context.[40] The techniques of using framing phrases and smart structural elements (both discussed earlier) may help AI tools 'understand' a case more accurately; but there is ultimately no guarantee they will succeed on each occasion.

In addition to concerns about accuracy, there are concerns about AI's ability to communicate tone. AI summaries may omit the very elements that signal ethical judgment or the court's nuanced voice. A sentence such as 'the court considers it inappropriate to express a concluded view on this issue in view of the current factual scenario' may be reduced to 'the issue was not decided'. Similarly, 'although the statutory language admits of competing interpretations, the court adopts the construction most consistent with precedent' may be flattened into 'the court applied precedent', thus erasing the deliberative tension. In such cases, a cautious and balanced judicial voice may be replaced by a blunt and mechanical summary.

AI can certainly serve as a supplementary aid in assisting reader comprehension, but it cannot and should not displace the judge's responsibility of writing judgments well. As argued in Chapter 1, judgment writing is much more than a declaration of outcome. It is a public account of reasoning. It ought to provide, as far as possible, a transparent trail from premises to conclusion. If the trails are habitually accessed only through technological reconstructions, we risk losing the very credibility that reasoned writing is meant to earn. Readers should be able to follow how and why a conclusion was reached *in the judge's voice*, not merely encounter the result narrated by an AI-generated interpretation.

CONCLUDING REFLECTIONS

The migration of judgment writing from print to digital platforms is not a mere change of medium. It reshapes how judgments are encountered, navigated, and understood. Typography, layout, and adaptive formatting are no longer peripheral concerns; they are integral to how judicial reasoning is received by parties, practitioners, and the public. A judgment that is visually accessible on a screen is more likely to be substantively accessible in meaning.

Yet the digital turn does not alter the fundamental responsibility of judges. The craft of judgment writing remains anchored in the principles espoused in this book. Technology can assist, whether through formatting tools, digital design principles, or even AI-enabled aids. But it cannot completely replace the judge's role (or, at least, not yet). The challenge, then, is for judges to write not only with an eye to the here and now but also to tomorrow: to audiences who will read judgments not only in libraries and law reports, but on global databases and all manner of digital devices.

AI tools will no doubt continue to assist readers in navigating legal texts, and these tools will get better. But that is no justification for judges to abdicate their responsibility to ensure that judgments are readable and comprehensible in their published form, whether in print or on screen. Judges must take responsibility for how judicial reasoning enters the world from bench to browser – a perfect segue into Chapter 8.

NOTES

1 That number is the character limit for a single post on X, formerly Twitter, where judgments may be reported, criticised, or celebrated shortly after release.

2 See e.g. Ziming Liu, 'Reading Behavior in the Digital Environment: Changes in Reading Behavior over the Past Ten Years' (2005) 61(6) J Doc 700.

3 Kara Pernice, Kathryn Whitenton and Jakob Nielsen, *How People Read on the Web: The Eyetracking Evidence* (Nielsen Norman Group 2014) 11, 54.

4 Pernice, Whitenton and Nielsen (n 3) 11, 79–80.

5 Pernice, Whitenton and Nielsen (n 3) 14–15.

6 See e.g. Liu (n 2); David Nicholas and others, 'UK Scholarly E-Book Usage: A Landmark Survey' (2008) 60(4) Aslib Proc 311.

7 'Discontinuous reading' has been defined as 'reading out of order', with the reader jumping back and forth in a text instead of following its linear and sequential order, while 'fragmented reading' refers to discontinuous reading of multiple texts of disconnected subject matters: Terje Hillesund, 'Digital Reading Spaces: How Expert Readers Handle Books, the Web and Electronic Paper' (2010) 15(4) First Monday <https://doi.org/10.5210/fm.v15i4.2762>.

8 Hillesund (n 7).

9 This proposition finds support in the speeches of Chief Justice Sundaresh Menon, who has argued that court and judicial reforms should be judge-led because judges are duty-bound to lead, are uniquely well-placed to lead, and it is in the interests of judges to lead. See Sundaresh Menon, 'Judicial Leadership: From Adjudication to

the Administration of Justice' (Speech to the Judiciary of the Republic of Rwanda, 14 March 2022) <https://perma.cc/85BP-NTXQ> paras 4–9; Sundaresh Menon, 'Judicial Leadership: Navigating Artificial Intelligence with Human Wisdom' (Keynote Lecture at the Singapore Judicial College's Judicial Executive Programme, 25 November 2025) <https://perma.cc/CPQ4-GJS7> paras 9–23.

10 Pernice, Whitenton and Nielsen (n 3).

11 Nielsen Norman Group, 'How People Read Online: The Eyetracking Evidence (2nd Edition)' <https://perma.cc/MP5H-98YP>

12 Pernice, Whitenton and Nielsen (n 3) 11.

13 Aries Arditi and Jianna Cho, 'Serifs and Font Legibility' (2005) 45(23) Vis Res 2926, 2927.

14 Jakob Nielsen, 'Serif vs Sans-Serif Fonts for HD Screens' (*Nielsen Norman Group*, 1 July 2012) <https://perma.cc/4QYB-K5L8>.

15 Nielsen (n 14).

16 See e.g. Katsumi Minakata and Sofie Beier, 'The Dispute About Sans Serif Versus Serif Fonts: An Interaction Between the Variables of Serif and Stroke Contrast' (2022) 228 Acta Psychol 103623; Arditi and Cho (n 13).

17 See e.g. 'Design for Readability' (*Harvard University Information Technology Digital Accessibility Services*) <https://perma.cc/BMN5-X94S>.

18 Pernice, Whitenton and Nielsen (n 3) 12.

19 Pernice, Whitenton and Nielsen (n 3) 158.

20 Pernice, Whitenton and Nielsen (n 3) 158, 346.

21 This point finds resonance in the American Psychological Association Style Guide: 'Headings' (APA Style, July 2022) <https://perma.cc/K3WZ-YVPT>.

22 'Design for Readability' (n 17).

23 An eye-tracking study has revealed benefits to non-liquid layouts, but liquid layouts are still considered generally the better choice: Pernice, Whitenton and Nielsen (n 3) 58.

24 Pernice, Whitenton and Nielsen (n 3) 108.

25 Ankit Singla, 'How Long Do Readers Stay on Blog Posts?' (*MasterBlogging*, 16 December 2024) <https://perma.cc/F7ZZ-P9AH>.

26 Therese Fessenden, 'Scrolling and Attention' (*Nielsen Norman Group*, 15 April 2018) <https://perma.cc/7FBH-QNJS>.

27 Fessenden (n 26).

28 See Chapter 4.

29 Pernice, Whitenton and Nielsen (n 3) 91, 307.

30 As discussed in Chapter 3.

31 Pernice, Whitenton and Nielsen (n 3) 12.

32 Pernice, Whitenton and Nielsen (n 3) 12.

33 Pernice, Whitenton and Nielsen (n 3) 91, 158.

34 See Chapter 3.

35 See text accompanying nn 3–4.

36 Eljas Linna and Tuula Linna, 'Challenges for Generative AI in Legal Reasoning' (*Cornell University arXiv Computer Science*, 2nd version, 24 January 2026) <https://doi.org/10.48550/arXiv.2508.18880>, s 3.2.3.

37 See, for instance, HyperWrite's Legal Case Summary Tool <https://perma.cc/547R-FVHW>.

38 One example is the 'AI Chat PDF' tool, which allows users to chat with their PDF files, as well as a wide variety of other file formats.

39 Nigel Toon, *How AI Thinks: How We Built It, How It Can Help Us, and How We Can Control It* (Transworld 2024) 59–60.

40 See Mousumi Akter and others, 'A Comprehensive Survey on Legal Summarization: Challenges and Future Directions' (*Cornell University arXiv Computer Science*, 29 January 2025) <https://doi.org/10.48550/arXiv.2501.17830>.

Reasoning and Responsibility – Authorship and AI

Eight

The public launch of ChatGPT in November 2022 may well be remembered as a watershed moment in the history of generative artificial intelligence ('GenAI') – a form of artificial intelligence (not to be confused with artificial general intelligence,[1] or predictive artificial intelligence[2]) that generates new information in response to a prompt in natural human language. More than 100 million people tried ChatGPT within two months of its launch,[3] myself amongst that number. I remember sitting at a desk in the Widener Memorial Library in Harvard University, typing in my first ever GenAI prompt, and doing a double-take as I wondered whether it was an actual human that had responded to me.

Shortly after the proliferation of ChatGPT and other GenAI tools powered by large language models ('LLMs') – massive artificial neural networks that are designed to process human language and generate new content – Professor Karim Lakhani of Harvard Business School observed:[4]

> *AI is not going to replace humans, but humans with AI are going to replace humans without AI. This is definitely the case for generative AI.*

In his 2025 lecture under the auspices of the Singapore Judicial College, Professor David Wilkins of Harvard Law School made a very similar observation to the Singapore judiciary:[5] GenAI may not replace judges, but judges with proficiency in GenAI may well replace judges without such proficiency.

GenAI has demonstrated an impressive ability in the legal space. Less than a year after its launch, ChatGPT ranked at the top 90th percentile of the United States' Uniform Bar Examination – a gruelling examination which involved not just multiple-choice questions but also open-ended essays.[6]

Little wonder, then, that judges around the world also began to experiment with using ChatGPT and other LLMs to assist them in judgment writing.

DOI: 10.4324/9781042017027-9

In England, for instance, Lord Justice Colin Birss asked ChatGPT to provide a summary of an area of law that he was familiar with. He then went on to use the generated summary in his judgment, later commenting that this had 'real potential' and was 'jolly useful'.[7]

In India, when deciding on a request for bail by a defendant charged with assaulting and killing an individual, a judge asked ChatGPT, 'What is the jurisprudence on bail when the assailant assaulted with cruelty?'[8] ChatGPT responded:[9]

> *If the assailants have been charged with a violent crime that involves cruelty, they may be considered a danger to the community and a flight risk. In such cases, the judge may be less inclined to grant bail or may set the bail amount very high to ensure that the defendant appears in court and does not pose a risk to public safety.*

The judge eventually denied the bail request. The judge later clarified that the use of ChatGPT was not an expression of opinion on the merits of the case and was 'only intended to present a broader picture on bail jurisprudence, where cruelty is a factor'.[10]

In the United States, a judge has suggested that it may be appropriate to consider whether and how LLMs may inform the interpretation of the ordinary meaning of words or phrases used in legal texts. This suggestion arose from a civil insurance case[11] where the issue was whether the installation of a ground-level trampoline in a backyard falls within the performance of 'landscaping', a term which was not defined in the insurance policy in question. Frustrated by the parties' arguments over the ordinary meaning of the term 'landscaping', the judge instructed his clerk to prompt ChatGPT and Google Bard as follows: 'What is the ordinary meaning of "landscaping"?' and 'Is installing an in-ground trampoline "landscaping"?'[12] Both LLMs answered the second question in the affirmative. Although the case was eventually dismissed on different grounds, the judge quoted the prompts and responses in his concurring opinion affirming the dismissal.[13]

Another instance of ChatGPT being used in a United States court is found in *Ross v United States*.[14] This was a criminal appeal concerning whether the government had proved that a dog left in a parked car on a hot day had been denied proper protection from the weather. The dissenting judge prompted ChatGPT (and asked three of his law clerks to run the same inquiry): 'Is it harmful to leave a dog in a car, with the windows down a few inches, for an hour and twenty minutes when it's 98 degrees outside?'[15] He then suggested that ChatGPT's confident answer to his question (stating that leaving a dog in a car under these conditions is 'very harmful'), although not a 'good proxy for what is, and isn't, common knowledge', was 'at least a point in favor of something being common knowledge'.[16] The majority responded by running a parallel experiment: it asked ChatGPT to estimate the value of a used Dodge Intrepid – a question whose answer was known from prior case law – and showed that ChatGPT's similarly confident response was wrong.[17] A separate concurrence then highlighted some considerations in the judicial and court use of AI tools.[18]

In China, the Shenzhen Intermediate Court unveiled an 'Intelligent Adjudication System' in 2024 which featured an LLM developed in collaboration with a Chinese company. This is reportedly the world's first instance in which a court has methodically utilised an LLM to aid judges in judging.[19] The process is essentially as follows: (a) the judge establishes and documents the facts of the case based on the evidence and court hearings (sometimes with the assistance of AI summarisation); (b) the judge identifies the disputed issues and indicates the decision on each issue; (c) the AI system generates reasoning based on the judge's decision on the disputed issues and established facts; and (d) the judge reviews and modifies the reasoning provided by the AI system to finalise the judgment.[20]

In the final stages of preparing this manuscript for publication, it was announced that the Superior Court of Los Angeles County had entered into a pilot collaboration with an AI company named Learned Hand.[21] Under this pilot collaboration, a select group of civil judges would have access to an AI software which can summarise motions and draft tentative rulings, but with purportedly extensive guardrails to fact-check and verify outputs. It is currently being tested on civil court motions such as motions for summary judgment and motions for approval of class-action settlements.[22] The Court's Presiding Judge indicated that the tool is being evaluated for how it may support judicial officers in managing a high-volume caseload, and also stated: 'Let me be clear – while this tool may enhance the way judicial officers review and engage with case files and information, it will not replace, or in any way compromise, the sanctity, independence, and impartiality of judicial decision-making.'[23] The use of the AI software has sparked diametrically opposing reactions from retired judges,[24] illustrating the difficult tensions that will have to be navigated as GenAI becomes part of the legal landscape.

I first experimented with using GenAI to facilitate judgment writing in late 2023. This was not for an actual judgment on my docket, as confidentiality concerns gave me pause. Rather, it was to prepare material for the foundational judgment writing programme that I teach at the Singapore Judicial College. ChatGPT proved adept at generating fictional judgment extracts to facilitate discussions on specific issues relating to judgment writing. The fictional nature of the extracts was particularly useful, as this ensured that class discussions focused on the writing rather than the writer. However, even used in such a context, I found that manual adjustments were routinely required to enhance the realism and real-world applicability of the fictional extracts. Careful human oversight remains critical when GenAI is used to facilitate the judgment writing process.

This chapter explores the tension between assistance and authorship in the age of GenAI, focusing specifically on the area of *judgment writing* (and leaving aside issues of AI-powered decision-making). It is neither a call to reject GenAI assistance nor a defence of traditional judgment writing processes. Rather, it is an invitation to reflect on what must remain human in the act of judgment writing. From the cognitive labour of drafting to the ethical boundaries of confidentiality, the authority of a judgment depends not only on how it is reasoned but also by whom it is shaped. This chapter concludes by suggesting some best practices for judges looking to use GenAI to assist with judgment writing.

THE APPEAL OF ASSISTANTS

Judgment writing is the core responsibility of the judge who adjudicates the matter. This responsibility is not discharged by mere approval on the judge's part. Personal and professional engagement is required. The judge must own the decision, ensuring that the eventual words reflect genuine judicial deliberation.

This does not mean that judges must work in isolation.[25] For instance, it is accepted in many parts of the world that judges may have the assistance of law clerks to assist in research and drafting tasks. Even if these clerks have personal opinions, these are always filtered through the judge's deliberation, revision, and ownership.[26] A survey (albeit dated) of 160 respondents who had served as law clerks in the United States from the 1930s to the late 1990s found that in relation to decision-making, the arguments of clerks were less important to the justices they served than factors such as the justices' jurisprudential philosophy, specific case facts, and precedent.[27] Singapore's justices' law clerk ('JLC') Programme reflects a similar ethos. While JLCs work closely with judges of the Supreme Court, their role is a supporting one. The deeply embedded expectation is that every Singapore judge engages actively with the material, provides guidance and thoughts to the JLC, revises drafts that the JLC may produce, and makes the final judgment the judge's own. Ultimately, the judgment must always be the judge's, shaped by the judge's reasoning, reflective of the judge's voice, and accountable to the judge's office.

Why the reference to law clerks in this chapter on GenAI? For present purposes, the point of comparison is especially salient. Analogies have been drawn between the assistance traditionally provided by law clerks and the use of LLMs in the drafting of judicial reasons.[28] For instance, a Colombian judge who used ChatGPT to produce portions of his judgment has claimed that the 'string of text that artificial intelligence provided me with could also have been provided to me by a clerk'.[29]

The appeal of LLMs in a judgment writing context is easy to understand. For the time-pressed writer (and judges very much fall into this category), it offers drafting on demand. It can tidy prose, suggest transitions, and summarise arguments. It can mimic judicial tone and reasoning. It can rephrase conclusions and suggest transitions with remarkable human-like (or even superhuman-like) fluency. In the near future, LLMs will be able to convincingly mimic specific judicial voices.[30] All that is required is that the user upload samples of the judicial voice in question as reference points for the LLM's digestion.

In this regard, I have enjoyed considerable success having various LLMs draft in the storytelling voice of Lord Denning MR.[31] As demonstrated in a judgment writing class that I taught in early 2026, Microsoft Copilot digested one of my published judgments in seconds and produced a Denning-esque introduction as follows:[32]

> *In this case, we are confronted with a tale as troubling as it is stark. Two men, having chanced upon two women rendered helpless by drink, chose not the path of decency but of predation. What began as an evening's idle wandering descended, step by deliberate step, into a grave abuse of trust and humanity. The accused, Mr X, did not merely follow where his companion led; he crossed the threshold of criminality with eyes open and conscience set aside. The law must speak plainly when modesty is outraged and vulnerability exploited, for such conduct strikes at the very fabric of civilised society.*

A few colleagues to whom I showed the extract were convinced that it came from Denning's own hand. What once demanded hours of careful crafting can, at least in outward form, now be produced in seconds. Jolly useful, in the words of Lord Justice Birss.

THE DANGERS OF USING GENAI IN JUDGMENT WRITING

In his well-known 1946 essay 'Politics and the English Language', George Orwell contended that 'if thought corrupts language, language can also corrupt thought'.[33] He was referring primarily to political writing of the day, but his warning carries broader lessons: that language, when used carelessly or mechanically, does not merely reflect poor thinking – it reinforces it. Stock phrases, dying metaphors, and pretentious diction, he argued, become obstacles to meaningful or original expression. Over time, the tools we use to express ideas begin to shape the way we form them. In Orwell's characteristically colourful exposition:[34]

> *A man may take to drink because he feels himself to be a failure, and then fail all the more completely because he drinks. It is rather the same thing that is happening to the English language. It becomes ugly and inaccurate because our thoughts are foolish, but the slovenliness of our language makes it easier for us to have foolish thoughts.*

While Orwell's critique focused on the stylistic decay of political prose, the deeper insight – that language and thought shape one another – remains strikingly relevant especially with the rise of GenAI. When expression becomes unthinking, the process of reasoning may begin to follow suit.

I outline four interrelated dangers that arise when GenAI is used to assist with judgment writing. These dangers are not speculative or peripheral – they strike at the heart of judicial authorship and the integrity of adjudication. They may be grouped under four headings, each capturing a distinct but connected risk: 'Unthinking Reasoning', 'Bull and Bias', 'Declining Automatons', and 'Compromised Confidentiality'.

Unthinking Reasoning

Even when LLMs produce text that sounds judicial, they do not 'think' or 'reason' like human judges (are expected to) do. To be sure, this is not simply a matter of waiting for LLMs to 'catch up'. LLMs are built on pattern recognition, serving as 'function approximators' that assist humans 'essentially, to autocomplete' tasks that humans otherwise had to do manually.[35] They do not possess functional models of the world and are incapable of even basic commonsense.[36] Alexander Lerchner's recent work on what he calls the 'Abstraction Fallacy' sharpens this point.[37] At the risk of oversimplifying his argument, Lerchner contends that LLMs function on symbols whose meaning is imposed by human agents, rather than grounded in any experience of their own. As such, LLMs engage only in 'extrinsic behavioral simulation' rather than 'intrinsic physical instantiation'.[38] Put another way, even if they can increasingly be trained to sound like human judges, they do not – and, in the view of some experts, never will – think or reason like them.[39] Rather, they function as 'stochastic parrots', repeating words and phrases that they have learnt through their massive datasets without actually understanding what they mean.[40] A caveat, however, is that this limitation reflects the architecture of current LLMs, which operate through statistical pattern matching rather than sequential, structured reasoning.

A recent joint study by AI and computer scientists from three countries found that LLMs offer promising capabilities for *supporting* legal reasoning tasks by *simulating* various aspects of legal reasoning.[41] Although they can respectably simulate rule-based reasoning and case-based reasoning, they currently face difficulties with abductive reasoning, or the imaginative and creative thinking that investigates multiple possibilities and plausibilities based on the available evidence. And because the LLMs 'can only approximate and not fully capture the complexity of real-world legal reasoning', the authors advocate approaching the integration of LLMs into judicial decision-making contexts with caution.[42] A GenAI-generated initial draft may read well, but it has not been properly reasoned through, if at all.

Because of this, inappropriate reliance on LLMs may impede the development of law and exercise of judicial discretion. Judicial reasoning involves the weighing of competing interpretations, the testing of normative boundaries, and the deliberate confrontation of ambiguity – none of which can be replicated by statistical prediction alone. This is particularly true in the common law system, where judges are called upon – particularly in new areas of law or in hard cases – to decide whether to update or depart from established rules. This requires 'a conscious, reasoned and forward-looking decision on whether and how our jurisprudence should evolve, having regard to the broader societal context which the law serves', instead of a 'backward-looking mechanical application of existing knowledge'.[43] The current GenAI tools cannot look forward in the same way that a judge can, as LLMs carry out their predictive functions by looking back at the data sets that they are trained with.

The exercise of judicial discretion is particularly nuanced in hard cases where there is no single answer, or where the case engages deeper questions of value and moral judgment.[44] In relation to the former, GenAI offers little assistance: probabilistic patterning is of limited use where courts must navigate grey areas or review a lower court's exercise of discretion.[45] In relation to the latter, it is the human experience that supplies the moral and social context within which rules and principles are derived and expressed.[46] A criminal sentence, for instance, 'expresses society's human response to the wrong drawn from collective value and feeling, through the judge',[47] while an exercise of judicial mercy rests on empathetic human sentiment.[48] On this point, a study found that GenAI, unlike human judges, was influenced by legal precedent but not by sympathy or other moral and social considerations.[49]

Before leaving the issue of 'Unthinking Reasoning', I flag the possibility that emerging 'agentic' AI frameworks (based on large *reasoning* models) may, in time, offer more structured forms of machine-assisted reasoning. These systems break a problem into smaller components, assign subtasks to specialised models, and then orchestrate the assembly of the outputs into a final answer. In theory, such architectures could impose a more disciplined reasoning workflow, particularly for routine or data-rich tasks such as the assessment of damages or the application of established benchmarks. But even here, the promise remains largely experimental. Decomposing a legal problem into discrete steps is not the same as exercising judgment about which steps matter, how they interact, or what weight to give competing considerations. The risk remains that an apparently well-structured chain of analysis masks the absence of genuine legal reasoning. At the time of this writing, agentic AI may assist with processes, but cannot replace the human capacity for interpretation, evaluation, and abductive insight.

Bull and Bias

Hallucinations are a well-known limitation of LLMs, from which even the latest legal specialist retrieval-augmented generation tools are not immune.[50] Examples abound of lawyers who relied on GenAI-generated hallucinated cases, one of the most embarrassing of which concerned an GenAI-generated submission which cited a criminal case falsely naming the judge himself as the accused person.[51] Some scholars have argued that 'hallucination' itself is a misleading term. Drawing on a term introduced into philosophical lexicon in 1986,[52] they suggest that such output is better understood as 'bullshit', defined as 'an utterance produced where a speaker has indifference towards the truth of the utterance'.[53] The 'bullshit' problem unfortunately cannot be resolved even if it were possible to curate a training set composed entirely of true propositions. For even if such a dataset could be assembled (which is, itself, improbable), a GenAI model would still be limited to extracting statistical patterns and remixing them when generating its output.[54] As a result, a significant proportion of its output would inevitably still be inaccurate.

While hallucinations (or 'bullshit') may be unavoidable, these are not the central risk to using them to assist in judgment writing. Responsible judges will check the accuracy of the GenAI output that they include in their judgments, and hallucinations (or 'bullshit') can often be identified and removed through diligence.

Far more dangerous and difficult to detect is the problem of bias. Unlike hallucinations, which are surface-level patterning errors, bias reflects the content of the model's training data, which in turn mirrors and amplifies the societal prejudices found in its datasets.[55] A key example of algorithmic bias in the justice setting is the controversy surrounding the Correctional Offender Management Profiling for Alternative Sanctions ('COMPAS') bail recommendation tool.[56] Similar concerns arise with modern LLMs, which may reproduce or entrench the ideological, cultural, or political leanings embedded in their training sources.[57] Compounding the difficulty is that biased GenAI output often appears entirely plausible, presenting itself as a 'natural' or 'acceptable' way to describe an issue, frame a dispute, or articulate a legal principle. Even if judges do not rely on LLMs for decision-making, their phrasing, framing, and suggested lines of reasoning may still seep into draft judgments, subtly shaping how judges characterise facts, evaluate credibility, or explain legal principles.

Declining Automatons

Socrates worried that the advent of writing would weaken our mental faculties, particularly memory, by outsourcing recollection to external marks rather than cultivating it within the mind. Centuries later, the abbot Johannes Trithemius lamented that the printing press might undermine the intellectual discipline fostered by handwritten manuscripts, fearing that ease of reproduction would erode the rigour of thought.[58] Each technological leap has carried the risk of deskilling – of mechanical convenience eroding human skill. GenAI is merely the latest instance of this familiar tension.

The real problem is not that GenAI may write poorly at times, for most judges will probably detect and rectify this before signing off on a judgment (much as they would for drafts submitted by law clerks). Rather, it is that GenAI will almost always write plausibly – producing sentences that sound judicial but which are not necessarily rooted in the judge's own reasoning. In such a situation, a judge may fall prey to automation bias.[59] Unfortunately, this creates a spiral in which 'a better LLM will only worsen the problem'.[60]

In the longer term, this may have nefarious effects on the judge's cognitive deliberation and the slow, effortful process by which meaning is made, ambiguity is wrestled with, and justice is shaped.[61] Recent research underscores this risk, for even highly educated persons and professionals are susceptible to the deskilling effects of over-reliance on GenAI tools.[62] This reliance may erode critical faculties and skills essential to adjudication, such as cognitive development, analytical precision, intellectual independence, and ethical discernment.[63]

A recent behavioural account of human–AI reasoning sharpens this concern. Researchers Steven Shaw and Gideon Nave argue that modern cognition increasingly unfolds within a *triadic* system in which external artificial cognition ('System 3') can displace or suppress the internal processes traditionally described as intuition ('System 1') and deliberation ('System 2').[64] Their empirical study showed that when GenAI assistance was available, participants frequently engaged it and often adopted its answers to logic and reasoning problems. Strikingly, they also became *more confident* in the correctness of those answers, notwithstanding that approximately half of the GenAI output in the experiment was incorrect. The presence of GenAI assistance 'displaced internal reasoning', shifting the locus of reasoning outward to the machine.[65]

In the judicial context, this dynamic underscores the risk that GenAI systems may gradually erode the judge's own deliberative engagement through the subtle habituation of relying on System 3 to do the cognitive lifting. This pattern of outward-shifted reasoning has been described as 'cognitive surrender' – a state in which the user not only consults GenAI, but relinquishes cognitive control and adopts GenAI's judgment as one's own.[66] Such cognitive surrender is more than automation bias. It reflects a 'deeper abdication of critical engagement'.[67] It marks the most acute form of the declining-automaton risk: the judge may retain formal authorship of the judgment, yet the underlying cognitive labour has been silently outsourced, with the habits of careful analysis and principled justification slowly atrophying through disuse.

Increasing reliance on GenAI tools may lead judges to operate primarily on the crutches of what might be called 'borrowed logic' – a term whose components are jointly and individually problematic in the present context. 'Borrowed' implies a relinquishment of ownership over thought (a real hazard for independence in judicial thought), while 'logic' refers not to logical judicial decision-making but pre-assembled probabilistic patterns that are divorced from the human, moral, and contextual realities.

Chief Justice of the Federal Court of Australia James Allsop warned:[68]

> *To mistake the machine for the Master will lead to the end of the spirit of the law as human and free. The danger is not the machine becoming human; it is the human becoming the machine.*

To this I would add that the danger may now take on an even more insidious form: not only the human becoming the machine, but the human becoming a mere appendix – present, but no longer essential to the body of judgment save to take responsibility for it.[69]

Compromised Confidentiality

The integrity of judicial reasoning depends not only on who writes, but on the conditions under which writing occurs. In this light, engagement with GenAI for the purposes of judgment writing must be governed not only by considerations of authorship and reasoning but also by a clear understanding of the confidentiality risks involved.

When judges or court staff use GenAI tools – particularly public or cloud-based models – to process case file materials or draft judgments, such sensitive information may be stored, transmitted, or even used to train future iterations of those models. The confidentiality implications turn largely on the terms of use of service. Public or free-to-use models often seek to retain user prompts and outputs for system improvement, including further training of the underlying model.[70] After all, these systems are data-hungry by design. Unless explicitly configured otherwise, they do not distinguish between public and confidential material. Some GenAI platforms also rely on human reviewers to review user data and input for content moderation purposes (amongst others). For instance, Google's Gemini App's privacy notice warned users not to enter confidential information that they would not want a human reviewer to see.[71]

It is thus unsurprising that many organisations, including technology companies, have banned their employees from using publicly available GenAI tools for work involving sensitive information.[72] At the same time, many institutions now subscribe to enterprise-grade GenAI services, which provide assurances that data will not be accessed for training or human review. Enterprise-grade models do reduce the confidentiality risks associated with public models but do not completely eliminate the risks. Any use of an external GenAI system still involves transmitting judicial material to a third-party environment outside the court's protected deliberative space.

This raises important questions. If a judge uses a GenAI tool to summarise a confidential affidavit, has that information now entered a third-party system? If a draft judgment is refined using an external model (whether public or enterprise-grade), has its content nonetheless travelled beyond the writing room?

As we have seen, the leak of a draft judicial opinion, albeit not through a GenAI platform, can cause much controversy and consternation.[73] The repercussions are not merely reputational. They strike at the integrity of the deliberative process itself. Judicial reasoning, especially in its formative stages, unfolds within a space of confidentiality that allows for hesitation, revision, and principled disagreement. The integrity of judicial authorship depends not only on the judge's reasoning but also on the confidentiality of the space in which that reasoning unfolds.

The Importance of Being Judicial

All four dangers just outlined individually and collectively pose a threat to judicial independence, integrity and impartiality and put public trust in the judiciary at risk. Ultimately, a judgment is not respected because it *sounds* judicial but because it *is* the product of judicial deliberation. It is authoritative not because it is *reasonable* but because it is *reasoned*. A judgment shaped by a tool rather than the judge's mind may well reach the right outcome, but it will have done so without the process that clothes the outcome with legitimacy. With the rise of GenAI, the judiciary must reaffirm that its legitimacy rests not just in *appearing* judicial but in *being* judicial.

TOWARDS A SET OF BEST PRACTICES

GenAI holds promise as a force for good in judgment writing. Its capacity to enhance clarity, structure, and linguistic precision is undeniable. However, the technological frontier remains a jagged one – one in which GenAI may be able to deliver excellent results in complex tasks but fail at comparatively trivial ones.[74] It may be 'a Ferrari in math but a donkey at putting things in your calendar'.[75] It may be 'remarkably capable, yet it struggles with many things a toddler can do'.[76]

Its promise must be tempered by principle. The challenge is not merely technical. It is also ethical and epistemic: how might judges harness modern GenAI tools without compromising the integrity of judicial reasoning and writing?

In this context, a 'Centaur' approach is preferable to a 'Cyborg' one, terms which I borrow from an illuminating study on how knowledge workers interact with GenAI tools.[77]

The 'Centaur' model, named after the half-human-half-horse creature of Greek mythology, envisions a principled division of labour between human and machine, with each contributing according to its strengths.[78] This can help preserve human authorship, ethical discernment, and cognitive engagement, while allowing GenAI to assist with pattern recognition, linguistic refinement, and structural coherence. Such a model retains the centrality of the human judge as author, with GenAI conceived of as a toolkit of different tools to assist the author with various tasks.[79]

In contrast, the 'Cyborg' model, named after science fiction's hybrid human-machine beings, is marked by deep integration and the intricate integration and intertwining of human and machine efforts.[80] In the context of judgment writing, a 'Cyborg' model risks eroding the deliberative clarity and institutional accountability that the task demands.

This distinction between 'Centaur' and 'Cyborg' is not merely academic or conceptual. It invites practical reflection. If the 'Centaur' model is to serve as a principled framework for judicial engagement with GenAI, it will be aided by concrete guidelines and principles.

In this regard, many courts around the world have established guidelines on the use of GenAI by litigants, the legal profession, and judges and judicial officers.[81] Many of the guidelines address legal and judicial work broadly. Judgment writing presents distinct cognitive and ethical demands which warrant specific consideration. I do acknowledge that the use of GenAI for editing or proofing draft judgments is currently expressly prohibited in certain jurisdictions.[82] However, there are many others which do not prohibit the use of GenAI to facilitate certain aspects of judgment writing. It seems inevitable that, eventually, GenAI or other forms of technology will be widely used to facilitate judgment writing. The more critical question, then, is *how* it should be used.

In my view, adopting a 'Best Practice' approach offers a valuable complement to the 'Guidelines' approach. While the latter generally focuses on boundaries (i.e., what judges must avoid), the former shifts the lens toward what judges should thoughtfully consider doing. This approach deepens the conversation by exploring the *how* of ethical and appropriate GenAI use rather than merely the *what not to do* – and in doing so, moves towards engaging directly with the craft and professionalism of judgment writing.

Against this backdrop, I suggest six best practices for a start: 'Start Human', 'Polish Structure', 'Red Team', 'Staged Review', 'Engineered Prompts', and 'Secure Tools'. There will, no doubt, be more to add to this list as judges begin using GenAI to assist in judgment writing.

Start Human

The first best practice is to preserve judicial ownership of the writing process by requiring the human judge to author the initial draft of the judgment. This approach is essential in ensuring that the judge retains control over the substance and direction of the reasoning process. By requiring judges to take the first step in drafting, we introduce what can be described as 'deliberate friction'[83] into the process.

LLM-generated draft judgments can offer conclusions that feel complete, coherent, and convincing. Sometimes, these conclusions are not what the judge would have independently reached absent the tool. The risk is particularly acute when it comes to preparing the initial draft of the judgment. Initial drafts often reflect the judge's incomplete but authentic understanding of the facts, the law, and how the case should be decided. In this regard, it bears emphasis that writing is more than a means of communication – it is, as Orwell has emphasised, also a form of thinking. The act of drafting forces the writer to confront ambiguity, test assumptions, and clarify conclusions.[84] When that process is outsourced to an opaque tool that offers ready-made fluency, we risk bypassing the very struggle that gives a judgment its moral and institutional force. Delegating the initial draft to a machine is not merely to outsource prose; it is to risk outsourcing responsibility.

I pause to note that even when judges rely on law clerks for research or drafting, the clerks never begin with a blank page. For decades, the judicial craft has required judges to supply their preliminary sense of the case – their views, analysis, and provisional conclusions – before any drafting or research begins. The introduction of LLMs does not justify a retreat from that discipline; if anything, it makes the judge's guiding (human) hand even more crucial.

Polish Structure

Next, judges should use GenAI for structural and linguistic enhancements, rather than to assist in (or worse, replace) the substantive decision-making process.

While the development of legal principles and the resolution of contested issues should remain human-led, GenAI can usefully support the organisation and phrasing of a draft. It may suggest headings, improve transitions, refine phrasing, and correct grammar – refinements that polish expression without altering meaning and decisions. This calls for careful context engineering: the deliberate shaping of GenAI's input environment, including prompt design and platform customisation, to ensure that its outputs remain within judicial boundaries. For instance, GenAI platforms can be customised to avoid crossing substantive decision-making boundaries (e.g., altering or suggesting changes to legal conclusions, interpretations, findings, or reasoning) or analytical integrity boundaries (e.g., to avoid removing qualifications or caveats or the weighing of competing principles). In the absence of platform-level customisation, simple prompt instructions such as 'Do not alter legal reasoning or conclusions' may – while rudimentary – nonetheless help reinforce boundaries and provide an additional layer of safeguard against substantive encroachment.

Red Team

The concept of the 'red team' was introduced by the United States military during the Cold War, with the term 'red' referring to the colour characterising the Soviet Union (or, more generally, an adversary).[85] Lawyers may be more familiar with the conceptual predecessor of the 'red team' – the 'Devil's Advocate' (*Advocatus Diaboli*), which served as an 'independent investigator and designated dissenter' who challenged the 'purported virtues and miracles for nominees for sainthood'.[86]

Applied in the present context, GenAI can serve as a form of 'red teaming': adopting an adversarial or sceptical stance to stress test a judge's reasoning and to stimulate critical reflection on a draft judgment. With the use of appropriate prompts, GenAI can raise counterarguments, surface overlooked precedents, and critique the clarity of a draft.[87] It can also flag inconsistencies between a draft judgment and other sources.

Used this way, GenAI can help sharpen a judge's reasoning by revealing blind spots or ambiguities, without becoming itself a substitute for judicial decision-making. It functions as a sounding board: not as a judge (or judge-replacement) but as a sparring partner. It is, in essence, an AI-powered Angus (if you have not encountered Angus, please see Chapter 6). Just as Holmes externalised his reasoning by speaking aloud to Angus, judges may externalise their reasoning by prompting GenAI to interrogate a draft.

As explored in the earlier section on 'Unthinking Reasoning', GenAI is not yet capable of reasoning in the manner expected of judges. But this does not prevent it from supporting the iterative development of ideas, mirroring the spirit of dialogic learning or the Socratic method. One must, of course, keep in mind the well-known tendency of GenAI models to please the user, known as a 'sycophancy' bias.[88] This tendency is caused by biases inherent in training data, limitations in current GenAI training techniques, and a lack of true understanding on the part of GenAI models.[89] Such a bias undermines the whole idea of a 'red team', but with proper prompt engineering (i.e., the crafting of user input into the GenAI platform) it may be possible to discourage or minimise sycophantic responses.[90]

GenAI holds much promise as a rough-and-ready 'red team' partner. Its use in judgment writing, however, requires careful boundary setting. The distinction between using GenAI to test a draft judgment and relying on it to shape or generate the reasoning is 'not a bright and clear one',[91] and there remains a risk of sliding from 'red teaming' into a form of abdication of judgment.

Staged Review (Human-in-the-Loop)

I know of judges who have tried to use GenAI platforms to review entire draft judgments at one go. In my view, it is better to run a draft judgment through GenAI in the form of a staged review process such that there is constant intervention from the judge throughout the process. The judge remains firmly the 'human-in-the-loop'. For instance, a judge may enter the 'Facts' section of the draft judgment into the GenAI platform and ask the platform to review the section for structural and linguistic issues. Upon receiving GenAI's suggestions or refined draft, the judge should review its input and ask: 'Does this still reflect my reasoning?', 'Has GenAI introduced subtle shifts in emphasis or interpretation?', 'Has it removed nuances that I ought to retain?'

As compared to an approach of relying on GenAI in a single pass, such a staged approach ensures that each group of GenAI suggestions is evaluated within the broader context of legal reasoning and factual analysis, thus preventing drift from the judge's intended meaning.

This staged iterative approach supports the 'Centaur' approach discussed earlier. Each checkpoint serves as a useful moment of reflection and, if necessary, recalibration. It also cultivates deliberative discipline. By pausing to review at structured intervals, judges engage in reflection about their own reasoning process. This can strengthen the quality of judicial analysis, as the checkpoints prompt judges to articulate why particular reasoning paths were chosen and whether they remain sound. Such staged review ensures that GenAI remains purely a tool of assistance rather than a substitute for judicial reasoning.

Engineered Prompts

Related to the idea of keeping the human-in-the-loop is the need for judges to cultivate working familiarity with prompt engineering. This refers to the disciplined technique by which GenAI systems are guided to produce outputs that are accurate and relevant to the judicial task. In a professional setting, prompts should not be treated as casual conversation. The fact that these systems accept natural language does not mean that any natural phrasing will yield reliable or legally appropriate results.

Prompt engineering requires the deliberate design of instructions, recognising that the form and structure of a prompt significantly influence the system's output. It includes context engineering: the careful organisation of background facts, constraints, and objectives so that the system's responses remain anchored to the judicial use case. By developing prompt or context engineering skills, judges strengthen their control over GenAI assistance. Effective prompting requires deliberate framing, precision, and awareness of how GenAI interprets instructions.

How does one structure a good prompt? This topic cannot be comprehensively canvassed in the limited confines of this book, particularly in such a rapidly evolving area of technology. That said, at the time of writing, a useful publicly accessible resource tailored specifically to the legal profession is the guide produced by Microsoft Corporation and Singapore Academy of Law.[92] The guide suggests that a good prompt has four components, which I adapt from and discuss briefly here.[93]

First, the 'Goal'. This should be stated at the very start of the prompt. Because most AI models process information sequentially, leading with a clear objective should achieve better results. The goal should be specific and action-oriented, using verbs such as 'draft', 'summarise', or 'rephrase'. Where the goal is complex, it is helpful to break the goal into smaller, prioritised steps.

Second, the 'Context'. This encompasses the background information the model needs to understand the task, including any constraints, the role of the writer, and the intended audience (for example, 'a judge writing a judgment' and 'lay readers of a court judgment'). Providing a few illustrative examples can further guide the model toward the desired style and structure.

Third, the 'Expectations'. This sets out how the output should be framed. It may include the required level of depth or detail, the tone (such as 'authoritative' or 'measured'), the format (for example, 'a written court judgment'), and any word limits (e.g., 'in 200 words', or 'in a single sentence'). Asking the model to work through the task step by step in a single prompt may help, although it is probably more effective to stage the review with a human-in-the-loop as suggested earlier.

Fourth, the 'Source'. It is generally advisable to supply reference material – whether an internal document (such as the 'Orientation Document' discussed in Chapter 6, and subject always to confidentiality considerations), statutory provisions, contractual clauses, or other relevant texts. Providing such material anchors the model's output and reduces the risk of error.

As an illustration, I uploaded to Microsoft Copilot a copy of the full decision in *Donoghue v Stevenson*[94] and entered a loosely engineered prompt, as follows:

> *Summarise this case.*

This is the unedited output:

> **SUMMARY OF DONOGHUE V STEVENSON (1932)**
>
> Facts
>
> - *On **26 August 1928**, Mrs May Donoghue consumed part of a bottle of ginger beer purchased by a friend at a café in Paisley.*
> - *The bottle, manufactured by **Mr Stevenson**, was opaque. After Donoghue had drunk some of it, a **decomposed snail** floated out.*

- She suffered **shock and gastroenteritis** and sued the manufacturer, despite having **no contract** with him (the drink was bought by her friend).

Procedural History

- The Lord Ordinary allowed the case to proceed to proof.
- The Second Division of the Court of Session dismissed the action, holding that the manufacturer owed no duty of care to a consumer with whom he had no contract.
- Donoghue appealed to the House of Lords.

Issue

Does a manufacturer owe a duty of care in negligence to the ultimate consumer of their product, even without a contractual relationship?

Decision

By a 3–2 majority, the House of Lords held YES: the manufacturer owed a duty of care to the consumer. The appeal was allowed.

Reasoning

Lord Atkin (Leading Judgment)

- Formulated the **"neighbour principle"**:
  - One must take reasonable care to avoid acts or omissions which one can reasonably foresee would be likely to injure one's neighbour.
- A "neighbour" is:
  - A person so closely and directly affected by one's act that one ought reasonably to have them in contemplation.
- A manufacturer who puts goods into circulation in a sealed container **intends** them to reach the consumer without inspection.
- Therefore, the manufacturer owes a **duty of care** to the ultimate consumer.

Lord Macmillan

- Emphasised that the categories of negligence are **never closed**.
- A manufacturer of food or drink intended for human consumption owes a duty to avoid causing harm.

Lord Thankerton

- Highlighted that the manufacturer's own actions (sealing the bottle, preventing inspection) created a direct relationship with the consumer.

Dissent (Lords Buckmaster and Tomlin)

- Argued that existing case law did **not** support such a duty.
- Warned against creating new categories of liability without precedent.
- Feared opening the floodgates to unlimited claims.

Legal Significance

- **Foundational case in modern negligence law.**
- Established the **general duty of care** based on foreseeability and proximity.
- Rejected the idea that liability required a contractual relationship.
- Became the cornerstone for the modern tort of negligence in the UK and Commonwealth jurisdictions.

I thereafter restarted the process, this time using a prompt that was engineered with the four prompt engineering components in mind:

> Summarise this case for insertion in the "Law of Negligence" section of a court judgment.Write as a judge, using clear, neutral, and simple language suitable for legal and lay readers.Write using one clear designation for each party throughout so the summary remains consistent and easy to follow. The summary must not exceed 150 words, identifying the nature of the claim, the main factual disputes, the legal questions to be determined, and the court's decision. Mention specifically the 'neighbour principle' that was established in this case.

This is the unedited output:

> Donoghue v Stevenson concerned a claim by the Consumer against the Manufacturer of a bottled ginger beer. The Consumer alleged that, after drinking from an opaque bottle purchased by a friend, she discovered the decomposed remains of a snail and suffered illness. The factual issue was whether the Manufacturer, who had no contract with the Consumer, owed her a duty to take reasonable care in the preparation of the drink. The legal question was whether the common law recognised such a duty to persons beyond those in a contractual relationship.The House of Lords held that the claim was legally relevant and could proceed. In doing so, it established the "neighbour" principle: that a person must take reasonable care to avoid acts or omissions which they can reasonably foresee would likely injure their "neighbour", meaning those closely and directly affected by their conduct. This principle became the foundation of modern negligence law.

The output of the properly engineered prompt is not perfect and must be further refined before it can be properly presented in a judgment as a summary of the seminal decision (as a parenthetical observation, it exceeded by two words my hard cap of 150 words). Nonetheless, it is clearly more fit for purpose than that of the loosely engineered prompt.

Prompt engineering is a learned discipline. Judges should expect to refine and iterate their prompts as part of obtaining reliable GenAI assistance.

Secure Tools

The final best practice concerns safeguarding confidentiality. While a published judgment is usually a public document, the path to its reasoning often involves sensitive material, internal deliberation, and provisional formulations that must remain secure. Using GenAI platforms to process such material risks unintended exposure or retention. Judges must therefore be discerning, not only in what tasks are delegated to GenAI, but *where* and *under what conditions* those tasks are performed. In many jurisdictions, judges are warned against entering information into GenAI platforms that is not already in the public domain.

Secure platforms that are specifically approved for judicial use offer a more appropriate environment. For example, Singapore judges and judicial officers have access to 'Pair', a secure suite of GenAI tools built collaboratively with OpenAI and Claude, which is cleared for use with data classified up to specified levels of sensitivity. A similar approach is taken in England, where judges have access to a secure version of Microsoft Copilot and an AI system developed in-house by His Majesty's Courts and Tribunals Service and the Ministry of Justice;[95] and in China (Shenzhen), where the 'Intelligent Adjudication System' is available for use only within the court system.[96] These offer models for how GenAI can be used without compromising confidentiality or institutional trust.

But what if a judge does not have access to any suitable secure GenAI platform? Even in that situation, it may be possible to use publicly available GenAI platforms if the judge restricts use to tasks which do not disclose deliberative material or identifying information.[97] For example, a GenAI platform can be used to suggest refinements to the headings of a draft judgment (without supplying the underlying content), to polish the phrasing of an anonymised draft judgment extract, or to provide red-teaming suggestions based on an anonymised account of the issue.

Protecting the integrity of the drafting process is not just a technical concern. It is essential to maintaining public trust and confidence in judicial decision-making.

CONCLUDING REFLECTIONS

As GenAI becomes more embedded in legal workflows, the judiciary must lead by example. In the context of judgment writing, judges must use technology with discernment and write with integrity. We must ensure that judgments remain recognisably and authentically human. For all its power and promise, GenAI must remain a servant of human judgment, not a substitute for it. After all, the authority of a judgment lies not in its fluency, but in its authorship. And that authorship must remain with the judge: a voice deliberating in public, accountable to the law, and entrusted with the power to decide.

I have advocated a 'Centaur' approach for the use of GenAI in judgment writing. This must never degenerate into what Cory Doctorow has described as the 'Reverse Centaur':[98] a configuration in which the machine becomes the head and the human merely the appendage, present chiefly to absorb blame when things go wrong. In such a model, the human-in-the-loop ceases to be an author and becomes a mere accountability sink.

Avoiding the 'Reverse Centaur' requires more than technical safeguards. It demands a principled commitment to preserving the human role at the centre of judicial reasoning and judgment writing. As observed by Chief Justice Sundaresh Menon, it is critical that we carefully consider the aspects of judging 'that remain, and *should* remain, a fundamentally human endeavour . . . [and] that must *endure*'.[99] Judgment writing is one such domain. Here, we must carefully safeguard the integrity of the voice of reason.

NOTES

1 Artificial general intelligence refers to AI that can perform most or all economically relevant tasks as effectively as any human. See Arvind Narayanan and Sayash Kapoor, *AI Snake Oil: What Artificial Intelligence Can Do, What It Can't, and How to Tell the Difference* (Princeton University Press 2025) 168.

2 Narayanan and Kapoor (n 1) 20.

3 Nigel Toon, *How AI Thinks: How We Built It, How It Can Help Us, and How We Can Control It* (Transworld 2024) 13.

4 Karim Lakhani, 'AI Won't Replace Humans – But Humans with AI Will Replace Humans without AI' *Harvard Business Review* (4 August 2023) <https://perma.cc/DCJ5-ZV6F>.

5 Professor David Wilkins has made this point in various lectures, including one delivered under the auspices of the Singapore Judicial College in July 2025.

6 Toon (n 3) 16.

7 Hibaq Farah, 'Court of Appeal Judge Praises "Jolly Useful" ChatGPT After Asking It for Legal Summary' *The Guardian* (15 September 2023) <https://perma.cc/ULT6-B8PX>. Lord Justice Birss had also clarified that he took full responsibility for his judgment, stating: 'I'm taking full personal responsibility for what I put in my judgment, I am not trying to give the responsibility to somebody else. All it did was a task which I was about to do and which I knew the answer and could recognise an answer as being acceptable.'

8 Pallavi Pundir, 'This Court Used ChatGPT to Decide Bail in a Murder Case' *Vice* (29 March 2023) <https://perma.cc/BMF3-LGFF>.

9 Pundir (n 8).

10 Pundir (n 8).

11 *Snell v United Specialty Insurance Company* 102 F 4th 1208 (11th Cir 2024).

12 *Snell* (n 11) (Newsom J).

13 See, for instance, the Appendix to Circuit Judge Newsom's opinion in *Snell* (n 11).

14 *Ross v United States* (District of Columbia Court of Appeals, 20 February 2025).

15 *Ross* (n 14) 37 (Deahl J).

16 *Ross* (n 14) 37 (Deahl J).

17 *Ross* (n 14) 11 (Shanker J).

18 *Ross* (n 14) 20–27 (Howard J).

19 John Zhuang Liu and Xueyao Li, 'How Do Judges Use Large Language Models? Evidence From Shenzhen' (2025) 16 JLA 238.

20 Liu and Li (n 19) 238–240.

21 James Queally, 'AI Pilot Program in LA County Courts Will Help Judges Craft Rulings in Some Cases' *Los Angeles Times* (18 March 2026) <https://perma.cc/DEC4-AKQH>.

22 Queally (n 21).

23 'Learned Hand Announces Partnership with Superior Court of Los Angeles County to Explore Emerging Technology to Support Judicial Officers' *BusinessWire* (18 March 2026) <https://perma.cc/97TW-9T7A>.

24 Retired Justice Arthur Gilbert responded with 'The horror! The horror!' – quoting the famous existential moment in Joseph Conrad's *The Heart of Darkness* – and also compared AI to 'an insidious worm burrowing in our brains to take over our ability to think for ourselves and the ability for judges to decide cases'. See Arthur Gilbert, 'The Horror! The Horror!' *Daily Journal* (6 April 2026) <https://perma.cc/ED96-YQST>. In contrast, former Chief Justice of the Michigan Supreme Court Bridget Mary McCormack argued that in the face of declining public confidence in the judiciary and huge psychological stress on judges due to the unmanageable caseload and backlog, AI is a tool which will help judges to decide matters faster and for cases to move faster through the courts, which will restore public confidence and allow judges to give cases the attention they deserve. See Bridget Mary McCormack, 'The Horror Isn't AI, It's What We're Doing without It' *Daily Journal* (13 April 2026) <https://perma.cc/6V4D-RBW7>.

25 See Chapter 6, 'The Consultation'.

26 The late US Supreme Court Justice John Paul Stevens compared the dynamic between judge and clerk to the relationship between lawyer and client: 'An interesting loyalty

develops between clerks and their Justices. It is much like a lawyer-client relationship, close and confidential. Like a lawyer, a clerk can't tell his client, the Justice, what to do. He can only suggest what can happen if he does or doesn't do something.' Or as a former clerk to the late US Supreme Court Justice William O Douglas put it: 'I always felt free to express my own opinions. Yet there was never any doubt as to who was the Justice and who was the law clerk. Justice Douglas's decisions and opinions were always his own, regardless of the magnitude of my assignments.' See Artemus Ward and David L Weiden, *Sorcerers' Apprentices: 100 Years of Law Clerks at the United States Supreme Court* (New York University Press 2006) 19, 20, 245.

27 Ward and Weiden (n 26) 245.

28 Richard M Re, 'Artificial Authorship and Judicial Opinions' (2024) 92(6) Geo Wash L Rev 1558.

29 Juan David Gutiérrez, 'ChatGPT in Colombian Courts: Why We Need to Have a Conversation About the Digital Literacy of the Judiciary' (*Verfassungsblog*, 23 February 2023) <https://perma.cc/5HNP-KEXS>.

30 Studies have demonstrated Generative AI's abilities to mimic writing style. See e.g. George Mikros, 'Beyond the Surface: Stylometric Analysis of GPT-4o's Capacity for Literary Style Imitation' (2025) 40(2) Digital Scholarship in the Humanities 587. The author prompted GPT-4o to analyse 15,000-word excerpts from texts by Ernest Hemingway and Mary Shelley and write 2,000-word short novels in the style of each author. The results were able to approximate surface-level stylistic features (see 597).

31 For instance, in *Miller v Jackson* [1977] QB 966 (CA), Lord Denning MR opened the judgment with the following: 'In summertime village cricket is the delight of everyone. Nearly every village has its own cricket field where the young men play and the old men watch. In the village of Lintz in County Durham they have their own ground, where they have played these last seventy years. They tend it well. The wicket area is well rolled and mown. The outfield is kept short. It has a good club-house for the players and seats for the onlookers. The village team play there on Saturdays and Sundays. They belong to a league, competing with the neighbouring villages. On other evenings after work they practice while the light lasts. Yet now after these 70 years a Judge of the High Court has ordered that they must not play there anymore. He has issued an injunction to stop them.'

32 This is the same judgment used to generate the 'writerly' introduction in Chapter 3 (on 'Setting the Scene: Crafting Engaging Introductions'). The reader is invited to compare the two to see if Microsoft Copilot was successful in generating a Denning-esque voice.

33 George Orwell, 'Politics and the English Language' (1946) 13(76) Horizon 252 (reproduced on *The Orwell Foundation*) <https://perma.cc/DT2S-8MNJ>.

34 Orwell (n 33).

35 Gary Marcus, 'LLMs Are Not Like You and Me – and Never Will Be' (*Marcus on AI*, 13 August 2025) <https://perma.cc/9MPK-DVPZ>.

36 Marcus (n 35).

37 Alexander Lerchner, 'The Abstraction Fallacy: Why AI Can Simulate But Not Instantiate Consciousness' <https://perma.cc/F7ZM-CJUE>

38 Lerchner (n 37).

39 Marcus (n 35).

40 Toon (n 3) 129.

41 Ha Thanh Nguyen and others, 'LLMs for Legal Reasoning: A Unified Framework and Future Perspectives' (2025) 58 Comput Law Secur Rev 106165 <https://doi.org/10.1016/j.clsr.2025.106165>.

42 Nguyen and others (n 41).

43 Sundaresh Menon, 'Judicial Responsibility in the Age of Artificial Intelligence' (Keynote Speech at the Inaugural Singapore-India Conference on Technology, 13 April 2024) <https://perma.cc/R45F-TFXU> para 9(b).

44 Ian Jackman, 'Some Reflections on the Use of Artificial Intelligence and Blockchain Technology in Insurance Litigation' (Speech Delivered at the Australian Professional Indemnity Group National Conference, 4 September 2025) <https://www.fedcourt.gov.au/digital-law-library/judges-speeches/justice-jackman/jackman-j-20250904> accessed 15 October 2025. The following passage is particularly illuminating: 'A further problem is that the more accomplished Generative AI is in filling gaps, the less sensitive it will be to the existence of a hard case, where the available legal materials do not lead logically to a single answer. The law has an open texture, the metaphor being of gaps between the warp and the weft in woven cloth. The law can never be entirely deductive. By their nature, rules have a core of certainty and a penumbrum of doubt. When a judge encounters a problem in that fringe of open texture, the decision will be guided by broadly evaluative reasoning, such as an assumption that the purpose of the rules which they are interpreting is a reasonable one, or that the rules are not intended to work an injustice or offend settled moral principles (HLA Hart, *The Concept of Law* (Oxford University Press 1961) 200). At times, a court is faced with a highly technical argument, which appears contrary to the real merits of the case. Judges, being human, then tend to ask themselves, "*Must* I accept that argument?" rather than "*Can* I accept that argument?" Judicial decisions can thus involve moral values or a choice between moral values, and morality does not always have a clear and discernible answer to offer (HLA Hart, *The Concept of Law* (Oxford University Press 1961) 200). The ultimate decision is neither arbitrary nor mechanical but involves an impartial and reasoned survey of the alternatives and a well-developed sense of judgment. Judges speak of "weighing" or "balancing" the competing interests. I do not think that artificial intelligence can replicate that kind of reasoning, nor in my view can it reliably predict the outcome in such a case. It certainly cannot dignify the person whose interests are at stake with a proper explanation produced by genuine intellectual engagement with the problem, rather than merely predicting the "correct" sequence of words as a large language model does.'

45 For this reason, United States Chief Justice John Roberts has predicted that 'human judges will be around for a while'. See John Roberts, '2023 Year-End Report on the Federal Judiciary' (Supreme Court of the United States) <https://perma.cc/3CWM-RSP2> 6.

46 James Allsop, 'The Legal System and the Administration of Justice in a Time of Technological Change: Machines Becoming Humans, or Humans Becoming Machines?' (Sir Francis Burt Oration, 21 November 2023) <https://perma.cc/7USX-HC3Z>.

47 Allsop (n 46).

48 John Tasioulas, 'Ethics of Artificial Intelligence: What It Is and Why We Need It' (2023 Elson Ethics Lecture, London, 4 October 2023) <https://perma.cc/G6FJ-MJZ7> 20.

49 Eric A Posner and Shivam Saran, 'Judge AI: Assessing Large Language Models in Judicial Decision-Making' (2025) Coase-Sandor Institute for Law & Economics Research Paper Series 25–03 <https://perma.cc/PLS4-6XK5> 28. Eric A Posner and Shivam Saran from the University of Chicago Law School replicated experiments in judicial decision-making conducted on 31 US federal judges and 91 law students using GPT-4o. The experiments required the subjects to decide on an actual case that had come before the International Criminal Tribunal for the former Yugoslavia, where the subjects were asked to assume the role of an Appeals Chamber judge and decide whether to affirm or reverse the trial chamber's decision to find the defendant guilty of aiding and abetting the planning, preparation or execution of crimes against Muslim civilians during the Yugoslavian civil war. Two factors were varied: whether the defendant presented as deserving of sympathy and whether precedent directs the judge to affirm or reverse. The results showed that GPT-4o was strongly affected by precedent but not by sympathy, which was similar to the results of the experiment involving law students, but the opposite of the experiment involving the judges, who were more influenced by sympathy. In addition, after training GPT-4o in various schools of judicial philosophy, the authors further prompted GPT-4o to decide the same experiment by applying one of five judicial philosophies. GPT-4o affirmed the conviction each time. The authors' discussion of the results is interesting as it poses the question of whether GPT is a superior judge in that it consistently follows well-defined legal rules and disregards non-legal factors. Conversely, the authors also consider that human judges 'are able to depart from rules when following them would produce bad outcomes from a moral, social, or policy standpoint'.

50 Varun Magesh and others, 'Hallucination-Free? Assessing the Reliability of Leading AI Legal Research Tools' (2025) 22 J Empirical Leg Stud 216.

51 This was a case in the Singapore courts: Natalie Skead and Justin Yeo, 'Judicial Education in a Brave New World' (2025) 59 Law Teach 666, fn 23. This case is also mentioned in Chapter 6, text accompanying n 6.

52 Frankfurt Harry, 'On Bullshit' (1986) 6 Raritan 2, 81–100. https://philpapers.org/rec/FRAOB-2.

53 Michael Townsen Hicks, James Humphries and Joe Slater, 'ChatGPT Is Bullshit' (2024) 26 Ethics Inf Technol <https://doi.org/10.1007/s10676-024-09775-5>.

54 Narayanan and Kapoor (n 1) 157.

55 Narayanan and Kapoor (n 1) 121.

56 The COMPAS bail recommendation controversy is an important reminder on how biases can operate invisibly within algorithmic tools. See Julia Angwin and others, 'Machine Bias: There's Software Used Across the Country to Predict Future Criminals: And It's Biased Against Blacks' (*ProPublica*, 23 May 2016) <https://perma.cc/CB7H-NVLV>, and the rejoinder at Anthony Flores, Kristin Bechtel and Christopher T Lowenkamp, 'False Positives, False Negatives, and False Analyses: A Rejoinder to "Machine Bias: There's Software Used Across the Country to Predict Future Criminals: And It's Biased Against Blacks"' (2004) 80 Fed Probat 38 <https://perma.cc/M5C9-VFQU>.

57 See e.g. Liu and Li (n 19); Rachel Courtland, 'The Bias Detectives: As Machine Learning Infiltrates Society, Scientists Grapple With How to Make Algorithms Fair' (2018) 558 Nature 357; Jon Kleinberg and others, 'Discrimination in the Age of

Algorithms' (2018) 10 JLA 113; Bushra Kundi and others, 'Artificial Intelligence and Bias: A Scoping Review' in Christo El Morr (ed), *AI and Society: Tensions and Opportunities* (Taylor & Francis Ltd 2022).

58 Ironically, Trithemius chose to print his treatise *In Praise of Scribes*, apparently because he thought he would gain a wider readership <https://perma.cc/4RBC-L5MD>.

59 Skead and Yeo (n 51) 18.

60 Liu and Li (n 19).

61 For instance, former US District Judge Katherine Forrest has emphasised the importance of the human judge's struggle to 'do the best we can', even if humans make errors and may not always have good motivations: Katherine B Forrest, *When Machines Can Be Judge, Jury, and Executioner: Justice in the Age of Artificial Intelligence* (World Scientific Publishing Co Pte Ltd 2021) 88.

62 In a multicentre observational study, highly experienced doctors, who had performed more than 2,000 colonoscopies each, were observed to have become 'less motivated, less focused, and less responsible when making cognitive decisions without AI assistance': Krzysztof Budzyń and others, 'Endoscopist Deskilling Risk After Exposure to Artificial Intelligence in Colonoscopy: A Multicentre, Observational Study' (2025) 10 Lancet Gastroenterol Hepatol 896. See also Nataliya Kosmyna and others, 'Your Brain on ChatGPT: Accumulation of Cognitive Debt When Using an AI Assistant for Essay Writing Task' (*Cornell University arXiv Computer Science*, 2nd version, 10 June 2025) <https://doi.org/10.48550/arXiv.2506.08872>; Michael Gerlick, 'AI Tools in Society: Impacts on Cognitive Offloading and the Future of Critical Thinking' (2025) 15(1) Societies 6.

63 It has been observed that 'AI may lead to a degradation of the legal skills that lawyers, judicial officers and judges are expected to possess. Analysis, retention, composition and formulation of arguments are all skills that need to be honed through daily use. With Generative AI potentially being used for drafting, research and analysis, the question is whether lawyers and judges will see abilities dulled through misuse': Aidan Xu, 'The Use (and Abuse) of AI in Court' (Speech at the IT Law Series 2025, Singapore, 30 July 2025) <https://perma.cc/GB5Q-7W8M> para 5.

64 Steven D Shaw and Gideon Nave, 'Thinking – Fast, Slow, and Artificial: How AI Is Reshaping Human Reasoning and the Rise of Cognitive Surrender' (2026) Wharton School of the University of Pennsylvania Working Paper <https://doi.org/10.31234/osf.io/yk25n_v1>.

65 Shaw and Nave (n 64). See the 'Discussion' Section at the end of 'Study 1: System 3 Influences Cognitive Reasoning'.

66 Shaw and Nave (n 64). See the Abstract.

67 Shaw and Nave (n 64). See the Abstract.

68 Allsop (n 46).

69 See, further, the reference to 'Reverse Centaur' in the 'Concluding Reflections' to this chapter.

70 For example, OpenAI states that user content is used to 'make our models more helpful', although it provides an option for opting out of this: OpenAI, 'How Your Data Is Used to Improve Model Performance' (28 April 2026) <https://help.openai.com/en/articles/5722486-how-your-data-is-used-to-improve-model-performance> accessed 30 April 2026.

71 See Google, 'Gemini Apps Privacy Hub' (8 April 2026) <https://perma.cc/5F3E-WPZN>.

72 See e.g. 'Samsung Bans Staff's AI Use After Spotting ChatGPT Data Leak' *The Straits Times* (2 May 2023) <https://perma.cc/DH2V-SFDV>.

73 See e.g. the leak of the draft majority opinion in *Dobbs v Jackson Women's Health Organization*, which sparked significant public and institutional reaction: Elizabeth Yoder, 'The *Dobbs* Leak as an Illustration of the Impasse Between Legal Ethics and Reality' (2023) 36(4) Geo J Legal Ethics 881.

74 Fabrizio Dell'Acqua and others, 'Navigating the Jagged Technological Frontier: Field Experimental Evidence of the Effects of Artificial Intelligence on Knowledge Worker Productivity and Quality' (2026) 37 Organ Sci 403, 405.

75 This quote is attributed to Anastasios Angelopoulos, CEO and cofounder of LMArena: see Deepa Seetharaman, Supantha Mukherjee and Krystal Hu, 'AI Promised a Revolution: Companies Are Still Waiting' *Reuters* (17 December 2025) <https://www.reuters.com/business/business-leaders-agree-ai-is-future-they-just-wish-it-worked-right-now-2025-12-16/> accessed 30 April 2026.

76 Narayanan and Kapoor (n 1) 47.

77 Fabrizio Dell'Acqua and others, 'Navigating the Jagged Technological Frontier: Field Experimental Evidence of the Effects of Artificial Intelligence on Knowledge Worker Productivity and Quality' MIT Sloan Working Paper 24–013 <https://perma.cc/WSV5-8BKV> 16.

78 Fabrizio Dell'Acqua (n 77) 16.

79 The computer scientist Randy Goebel has suggested that instead of aspiring to a single 'godlike' LLM that can render perfect decisions and legal arguments, he foresees many separate AI tools being employed for different types of legal tasks. See Riley Tjosvold, 'Is AI Ready for the Courtroom? New Framework Tackles the Technology's Biggest Weaknesses' (*TechXplore*, 28 October 2025) <https://techxplore.com/news/2025-10-ai-ready-courtroom-framework-tackles.html> accessed 30 April 2026. Professor Goebel's approach seems a sensible one for judges to adopt.

80 Fabrizio Dell'Acqua (n 77) 16.

81 For instance, the New Zealand judiciary issued 'Guidelines for Use of Generative Artificial Intelligence in Courts and Tribunals' (7 December 2023) <https://perma.cc/6FG7-MSK5>. In Australia, there are multiple sets of guidelines – the Chief Justice of the Federal Court of Australia issued a media statement relating to the use of Generative AI: 'Notice to the Profession: Artificial Intelligence Use in the Federal Court of Australia' (29 April 2025) <https://www.fedcourt.gov.au/law-and-practice/practice-documents/notice-to-profession/29-april-2025> accessed 30 April 2026; the Queensland Courts launched (on 13 May 2024) and recently issued a revised version (on 15 September 2025) of 'The Use of Generative AI: Guidelines for Judicial Officers' <https://perma.cc/CC4Z-6C7G>; the Chief Justice of New South Wales issued 'Guidelines for New South Wales Judges in Respect of Use of Generative AI' (21 November 2024) <https://perma.cc/QN52-6FCR>; the Supreme Court of Victoria likewise issued 'Guidelines for Litigants: Responsible Use of Artificial Intelligence in Litigation' (May 2024) <https://perma.cc/A2Q8-XE68>.

82 In New South Wales, the guidelines categorically state, 'Gen AI should not be used for editing or proofing draft judgments, and no part of a draft judgment should be submitted to a Gen AI program': see 'Guidelines for New South Wales Judges in

Respect of Use of Generative AI' (n 81). A similar position is taken in the Queensland courts – AI tools are not to be used for decision-making or to develop or prepare reasons for decision, as 'the development and expression of judicial reasoning must be done by the judicial officer themselves': see 'The Use of Generative AI: Guidelines for Judicial Officers' (n 81).

83 I first came across this term, in the context of judgment writing, in comments made by Professor Jungpil Hahn, a professor in the Department of Information Systems and Analytics and the Provost's Chair Professor at the School of Computing at the National University of Singapore.

84 See Chapter 1 (on 'Encouraging Accuracy').

85 Micah Zenko, *Red Team: How to Succeed by Thinking Like the Enemy* (Basic Books 2015) in the chapter 'Two: Origins: Modern Military Red Teaming'.

86 Zenko (n 85), in the chapter 'Introduction'.

87 Xu (n 63) paras 20, 23. See also Aidan Xu, 'Designing Digital Justice: Access, Effectiveness, and Confidence' (Speech at the Seminar 'The Expanded Scope of Dispute Resolution in Civil Justice', Singapore, 23 April 2026) <https://perma.cc/63DW-EU6N> para 31. The authors of the study of the Shenzhen 'Intelligent Adjudication System' have also suggested that the workflow of judge–AI interactions could be restructured such that the LLMs are required to present arguments both supporting and opposing the judges' initial decisions, with the judges then instructed to evaluate both sides of the arguments before coming to a final decision to mitigate the risk of confirmation bias: see Liu and Li (n 19) 252.

88 Lars Malmqvist, 'Sycophancy in Large Language Models: Causes and Mitigations' (Computing Conference 2025 (forthcoming)) <https://doi.org/10.48550/arXiv.2411.15287> 6–7.

89 Malmqvist (n 88) 6–7.

90 Malmqvist (n 88) 3.

91 Xu (n 87) para 32.

92 Singapore Academy of Law and Microsoft Corporation, 'Prompt Engineering for Lawyers (2nd Edition): Leveraging Generative AI in the Legal Profession' (*Singapore Academy of Law*, 2025) <https://perma.cc/U96F-9RML>.

93 'Prompt Engineering for Lawyers' (n 92) 3–5.

94 *Donoghue v Stevenson* [1932] AC 562 (HL), 580.

95 Colin Birss, 'Legal Professional Privilege in the Age of AI' (Speech to the City of London Law Society, 22 April 2026) <https://perma.cc/28ZS-3H2B> para 11.

96 Liu and Li (n 19) 238.

97 *Ross* (n 14) 25 (Howard J).

98 Cory Doctorow, 'AI Companies Will Fail: We Can Salvage Something From the Wreckage' *The Guardian* (18 January 2026) <https://perma.cc/P53C-GDG3>.

99 Menon (n 43) para 6.

Epilogue

When the Writing Is Done

When the writing is done and the judgment released, it stands on its own. It is both a conclusion and a beginning, resolving the dispute (at least for now) while simultaneously entering the world and the stream of legal history. It may be read by the parties, cited by counsel, critiqued by courts and academics, studied by students, and scrutinised – sometimes fiercely - by the press and the public. It may be embraced, challenged, misread, or forgotten. Yet it remains part of the judicial record. Not just of a case, but of a court, a system, a society, or even of humanity.

Written judgments endure. They are the most visible expression of judicial reasoning. They guide future cases, shape legal doctrine, and influence how the public understands the law. They may comfort those who seek justice, or confront those who wield power. And over time, they form a corpus that either strengthens or erodes public trust in the judiciary.

Writing good judgments requires practice. It is a discipline honed over time, through repeated effort and reflection. Each draft is an exercise in judgment as much as in writing. The cost is measured in hours of revision, and in the patience to cut, reshape, and refine. That cost is rarely visible to the reader, who sees only the finished headings, paragraphs, and flow of prose. They do not see the struggle over order, the decision of what to omit, or the drafts where a long paragraph became two short ones. They do not see the detours – often written with care and deleted with wistfulness – that never reach the published page. This hidden labour is what makes judgment writing not merely a technical exercise, but a practice of integrity and a labour of love for the law and for justice.

Judgment writing is not just a matter of clarity or efficiency. It is a matter of integrity. The words we choose, the tone we strike, and the reasoning we offer are not just stylistic choices. They should reflect the core values of judgment writing as discussed in Chapter 1: fidelity to law and

DOI: 10.4324/9781042017027-10

fact, integrity of reasoning, respect for the law and for people, and institutional stewardship. The question is not only whether the judgment is correct. It is also whether the judgment reflects the kind of judge we aspire to be and the kind of institution we serve.

When the writing is done and the judgment is released, what remains is not just a record of decision, but a testament to the enduring duty of every judge: to speak, in every written judgment, with the voice of reason.

Selected Bibliography

Berry E, *Writing Reasons: A Handbook for Judges* (6th edn, LexisNexis Canada 2025)

Cohen M, 'When Judges Have Reasons Not to Give Reasons: A Comparative Law Approach' (2015) 72 *Wash & Lee L Rev* 483

Cole G and others, *Making Decisions Judicially: A Guide for Decision-Makers* (Hart Publishing 2022)

Dell'Acqua F and others, 'Navigating the Jagged Technological Frontier: Field Experimental Evidence of the Effects of Artificial Intelligence on Knowledge Worker Productivity and Quality' (2026) 37 *Organ Sci* 403

Flowers B, 'Madman, Architect, Carpenter, Judge: Roles and the Writing Process' (1981) 58 *Language Arts* 834

Hicks MT, Humphries J and Slater J, 'ChatGPT Is Bullshit' (2024) 26 *Ethics Inf Technol* <https://doi.org/10.1007/s10676-024-09775-5>

Ho HL, 'The Judicial Duty to Give Reasons' (2000) 20 *Leg Stud* 42

Menon S, 'Judicial Responsibility in the Age of Artificial Intelligence' (Keynote Speech, Singapore–India Conference on Technology, 13 April 2024) <https://perma.cc/R45F-TFXU>

Narayanan A and Kapoor S, *AI Snake Oil: What Artificial Intelligence Can Do, What It Can't, and How to Tell the Difference* (Princeton University Press 2025)

Raymond J, 'The Architecture of Argument' (2004) 7 *The Judicial Review: J Jud Comm New South Wales* 39

Shaw SD and Nave G, 'Thinking – Fast, Slow, and Artificial: How AI Is Reshaping Human Reasoning and the Rise of Cognitive Surrender' (2026) Wharton School of the University of Pennsylvania Working Paper <https://doi.org/10.31234/osf.io/yk25n_v1>

Sheppard J, 'The "Write" Way: A Judicial Clerk's Guide to Writing for the Court' (2008) 38 *U Balt L Rev* 73

Toon N, *How AI Thinks: How We Built It, How It Can Help Us, and How We Can Control It* (Transworld 2024)

Index

Note: Underlined page numbers indicate a box on the corresponding page.